CONFESSION
OF A THUG AND A GENTLEMAN

CONFESSION
OF A THUG AND A GENTLEMAN

Darren Jaz Vincent

Confession of a Thug and a Gentleman

Copyright © 2018 by Darren Jaz Vincent. All rights reserved.

No part of this publication may be reproduced, stored in a retrieval system or transmitted in any way by any means, electronic, mechanical, photocopy, recording or otherwise without the prior permission of the author except as provided by USA copyright law.

The opinions expressed by the author are not necessarily those of URLink Print and Media.

1603 Capitol Ave., Suite 310 Cheyenne, Wyoming USA 82001
1-888-980-6523 | admin@urlinkpublishing.com

URLink Print and Media is committed to excellence in the publishing industry.

Book design copyright © 2018 by URLink Print and Media. All rights reserved.

Published in the United States of America

ISBN 978-1-64367-148-2 (Paperback)
ISBN 978-1-64367-149-9 (Digital)

1. Non-Fiction/Self-help
2. Biography
05.12.18

CONTENTS

Chapter 1: Fighting For My Life 7
Chapter 2: Being A Single Mother In The 'Hood 13
Chapter 3: Being A Man At Fourteen 17
Chapter 4: The Law In The 'Hood 21
Chapter 5: The Sexual Abuse 29
Chapter 6: Becoming A Father 34
Chapter 7: Trying To Understand My Anger 39
Chapter 8: Family Influence In The 'Hood 46
Chapter 9: Religious Influence In The 'Hood 52
Chapter 10: Love In The 'Hood 56
Chapter 11: Trying To Stop Fighting 69
Chapter 12: Learning To Be Submissive 87
Chapter 13: From Thug To Gentlemen 91
Chapter 14: Books Changed My Life 96
Chapter 15: The 'Hood Comes With No Credibility 101
Chapter 16: Learning To Follow 106
Chapter 17: Learning To Lead 111
Chapter 18: And You Still Treat Me As A Thug 121

CHAPTER 1

FIGHTING FOR MY LIFE

Blood flowed down my face. I wanted to take action, but I couldn't move. It was as if an invisible, dominant being was holding me. I was conscious. I could see and hear everything around me, even though the heavy blood that dripped down the right side of my face blurred my vision and limited my hearing.

"A friend yelled, "Let's get 'em, Jaz. I got your back!"

Other people in the bar stumbled over each other, rushing towards the exit. What about me? Why was I still standing in one spot? Where was my brother? Was I going to bleed to death? Who hit me?

I heard a voice, but I couldn't see where it was coming from. The voice screamed, "It was Me who gave you strength to make it this far! It was Me who kept you out of harm's way! It was Me who kept you from spending your life in jail! Most of all, it was Me who sheltered you from death! If you don't listen this time, you're on your own!"

My mind raced into the past. I had participated in hundreds of fights in my lifetime—professional matches, brawls at school, in bars, and on the streets. For the most part I was victorious, apart from a few broken bones, scars, and minimal jail time. Up to this point in my life I had convinced myself that I was a great fighter. I was strong and had tremendous speed. I was cunning for a person with no criminal record, and I was still healthy.

In a split second, that night at the bar, that voice sent me back in time. I thought about how I had gotten to this night. How did I come to be standing in a bar feeling as if half my face had been ripped off? My thoughts took me back to 1980. I was seven or eight years old, riding my Evel Knievel, red-white-and-blue Chopper Big Wheel on the sidewalk of Fourteenth Street in Niagara Falls, New York.

The front wheel, connected by two chrome bars that seemed to glisten in the sun, stretched out about three feet in front of me. Most of the other kids had normal Big Wheels made of nothing but plastic that fell apart after a few months. Even though we were poor and living in the "the hood", my mother loved to get me things the other kids didn't have. In the "hood" we called this practice living "ghetto fabulous."

I remember one day when I was wearing a special shirt my mother had bought me. She probably thought it made a positive fashion statement about her son but looking back I'm not sure that was the case. It was an orange-white-and-blue striped, short-sleeve shirt and I proudly sported my afro with it. At the time the shirt didn't bother me since it was how most young kids dressed at that time, but now when I look back at old photos, that shirt really looked horrible.

Anyway, that day a man named Steve was arguing with my Godmother Joyce who lived next door to us. I slowly pedaled my Big Wheel out of my yard and headed toward the commotion. As I got closer to Steve and Joyce, I pedaled faster and then purposely ran over Steve's foot. When I looked up and smiled, he spit on me. Joyce immediately attacked Steve with uncontrollable rage. It was a rage I was familiar with since I had witnessed my mother attack men like that on a few occasions. It always amazed me. My mother reminded me of a wolverine when she attacked. She was fast and aggressive even as she seemed to be in control and aware of her surroundings.

Soon after Joyce's fight I returned home. The moment I walked into the house my mother screamed, "Go straight to your room and take off your clothes!"

It was clear to me what was going to happen. Though I couldn't figure out what I had done wrong, I was about to get a beating. I stripped off my clothes down to my dingy white underwear. I was scared. Actually I was horrified. I shivered and paced until I heard a creak in the floor and the rattle of a belt buckle. My mother was walking through the living room that led to my bedroom. I leaped on the other side of my bed, out of reach, but with the wall behind me. My mother entered the room.

"Come over here," she demanded.

I paused and began to cry. I shook my head no.

She demanded again, "Now!"

I was so scared I felt as though I was going into shock. I walked reluctantly around the bed toward her.

"Please, Ma, I'm sorry. Don't hit me. I won't do it again," I cried.

Her face was motionless, but full of anger. She took a stance preparing to strike. As the belt went up, I dove to the floor as if she had already hit me. The first real hit struck like a bullet. I screamed.

She hit me faster and faster as she yelled, "Didn't I tell you to stay out of grown folks' business?"

"Yes, Ma," I cried. "I won't do it again."

The pain was intolerable, but I had enough strength to think, I can't wait 'til this is over.

Suddenly, after about the fifth or sixth strike, she stopped. Still crying, I crawled away from within striking distance. She hit me three more times, demanding that I stop crying. I couldn't understand why she was telling me to stop crying since it hurt.

Finally, she stopped beating me. "What did I tell you about messing with adults.

I was too scared to answer. Either way, there was a great risk of getting hit again. There was no right answer, not even the truth.

"You told me stay out of grown folks' business," I cried.

By this time, I was in a ball trying to protect the areas that she'd hit the most, mainly my arms. While she was hitting me I constantly reached up in an effort to limit the belt to only hitting my arms.

"Then why did you go over there and mess with Joyce and Steve?" she yelled.

"I don't know, Ma," I cried. Wrong answer! She struck me again. She demanded an answer to a question that I didn't have a clear understanding of how to answer, so I lied. "He yelled at me," I said.

"If I find out you're lying, you're getting another whippin'," she proclaimed. She then turned and walked out of the room. I didn't move for about ten minutes, shivering in pain. My arms were red and branded with imprints from the belt. The belt was thick with big holes. I actually felt fortunate that she didn't use one of her thin belts; they hurt more. I couldn't help but think that I had just set myself up again for another whippin' by lying.

I fell asleep in the corner of my room. Late that night I was awakened by my mother. She delicately helped me off the floor. She looked heartbroken. She picked me up in a nurturing way, as if I were 3 years old. She held me close to her chest. My mother didn't say she was sorry often, but this was most likely her way of saying it. After a few seconds she ordered me to put on my pajamas and get into bed.

The following morning, I was awakened by my mother's voice. "Get ready for school," she said.

I rushed to get my clothes together. After washing up and putting on my clothes, I yelled across the small apartment, "I'll see you later, Ma."

I tried to get to the door before I heard her yell, "Come here, boy, let me see what you got on."

I walked toward her bedroom with my head down. My mother wanted to make sure I had on my snow suit. She would also put a massive amount of Vaseline on my face. She claimed it protected my face from the cold. After leaving her room I glared into the glass on the stove and witnessed my face shining like the sun.

To get to my bus stop I had to cross a field with prickly bushes and high weeds that grew between two old buildings with boarded windows. When the weather was warm, I looked for grasshoppers as I passed through this area, while at the same time trying to avoid the sting of the prickly leaves on the bushes.

Next I had to cross an alley that was paved with rocks and garbage. The alleyway was so different during the daytime. Kids were told to stay away from this alley. At night, only bums, drug addicts, and drug dealers roamed that alley. The abandoned buildings looked haunted and behind every garbage can and dumpster you could hear noises from animals that owned their spot making it even scarier. We all knew a lot of the violent crimes took place in this area.

Many of the kids were already at the bus stop when I got there, pushing and teasing each other. As the yellow bus approached, a boy about my age shoved me in order to get on the bus first. I felt something boil inside of me as he pushed me aside. He looked back at me, and I gave him a look, much like how my mother looked at me before I got a whippin'. I calmly walked up the stairs to the bus. As I passed his seat I paused, looked him in the eye and said, "You're going to pay for pushing me."

I stayed silent throughout the forty five minute bus ride to 66th Street Elementary School, edgy and anxious for the bus to stop. I stared out the window until we finally reached the school. I made sure I was close behind the boy as he got off the bus. He had walked about two feet from the bus when I leapt off the last step and onto his back. We rolled into the grass and then into a pile of mud. I punched him violently. With every blow, I seemed to become angrier. I felt almost like an enraged animal.

I was direct, aggressive, and fearless. I hit him repeatedly with everything I had.

I barely felt the hand that grabbed me from behind. I was still in a trance, overwhelmed by my emotions. It was the Principal pulling me off him. The boy stood up, embarrassed. He wasn't crying. I could tell he was doing his best to avoid looking at me. He looked around as if he was counting how many people had witnessed the fight. The principal held me tight around my bicep and pulled me into the school. The crowd gawked at me as if I was a hero. Some cheered me on, "You the man! You the man!"

My emotions shifted from anger to fear as I realized the Principal was going to do what I dreaded more than anything; he was going to call my mother. It would take my mother at least an hour to get to the school since we didn't have a car and she would have to find a ride. I wanted to express to the Principal how mad I was at him for telling on me so I began kicking his desk. He ignored me while filling out some paperwork. I bolted from the chair and ran out of his office. I ran through the hallways and ended up in the secluded boys' locker room. Soon afterwards I heard the door open. I had nowhere to hide. Again, it was the Principal. He had a circular paddle in his right hand. It was the same kind people used to play ping-pong. He grabbed me again and put me over his lap with my stomach on his knees. I kicked and kicked, but couldn't get loose. He struck me about four times, leaving a painful bruise on my butt. I screamed and yelled as he walked me back down to his office.

My mother arrived momentarily after we got to the office. "Why is my son crying?" she asked, the second she walked into the office.

The principal admitted to whippin' me. My mother called him every word that I had been told not to say. I was shocked that she was upset with him for hitting me. Still, that night, I got a beating for lying the night before, fighting, getting my clothes muddy, getting suspended, and running from the Principal.

Confusingly, on many occasions my mother would somehow show up on site while I was fighting. If I was caught losing, she would ask me why I was fighting. If I was able to convince her that it wasn't my fault, she demanded that I fight the boy again. She would threaten me, "If you lose, you have to answer to me." If she wasn't on the scene, and had heard that I lost a fight, she would actually wake me up to find the challenger and force me to fight him again I recall standing in front of a big poster in my bedroom. The background was black and it had colorful animals on it shaped like the alphabet. I stood in front of the poster crying and trembling. My mother stood in front of me pointing at the small letter "b." She had a belt in her hand and a no-tolerance look on her face.

"What is this?" she asked.

"It's a 'd,'" I cried.

She hit me with the belt. Scared for my life, I changed my answer.

"It's a 'b.'"

She moved to other letters. I did well until she asked about the small letter "d." "What is this?" she demanded.

"It's a 'b,'" I cried. Again she hit me with the belt.

And again, I changed my answer, "It's a 'd.'"

I wasn't doing this for the pleasure of being hit. I had a problem with the small letters "b" and "d," especially under this type of pressure. The quizzing and beating went on for about twenty minutes, but it felt like hours. When my mother left the room I could see the details of the belt on my arm again.

This type of behavior was normal in my home. I was scared of my mother. She was trying to teach me to be tough and smart, but the beatings were creating a monster. I was conflicted. On one hand, I was being taught to stand up for myself, make the right choices, and do it without getting mad, but on the other hand, I was taught not to stand up for myself or she would beat me.

I recall standing up to my mother once. I had to be about 9 years old. My Aunt Ellen was having a baby shower at our house. Some twenty family members came out to celebrate and give Ellen gifts for her unborn baby. My Aunt Claudia was sitting on the couch with a glass of ice in one hand and a cigarette in another. Every couple of minutes she would grab a piece of ice and put it in her mouth. The sound she made crushing the ice in her mouth sent chill bumps up my arm. Still when someone chews on ice, I get chill bumps.

"Can you stop making so much noise with that ice?" I asked, boldly.

I'm not sure why I said that to Claudia so boldly because she was one of my favorite aunts.

Somehow my mother heard me from the other room. She approached me with a "you-know-better" look on her face.

"Leave grown folks alone," she snapped.

I looked around the living room and it seemed like everyone was staring at me. I felt ashamed.

Obstinately, I responded, "No!" shocking even myself. I was sure she wouldn't do anything to me with so many people around. But I was wrong, this was the fearless Linda Camp. She carried switches in her pocketbook and was known to grab a branch from a tree while walking down the street. She would swiftly draw her switch from her belongings in a department store and whip me in front of a bunch of strangers. I should have known she wasn't scared to strike me in front of relatives.

This time she came at me with so much rage that I took off running. As I jetted up the stairs, I heard footsteps behind me. I stumbled into my room and before I could look back she was already on top of me. In that short period of time she had managed to grab a weapon. She whacked me over and over with a hanger.

"Help! Help me somebody, please! Help!" I yelled.

But no one responded. It seemed like a long period of time passed and she was still beating me. Why wasn't anybody helping me? Finally, three people ran upstairs and grabbed her. I will never forget the look on her face as relatives pulled her away. There was more than anger that contorted her face, it was rage. She tried to pull herself loose to attack me again. Years later as a young adult, whenever I read about a young African-American man who went off in anger for what seemed like no reason, I was reminded of my beatings. I wondered if maybe he learned this violence from being beaten the way I was as a youth.

CHAPTER 2

BEING A SINGLE MOTHER IN THE 'HOOD

When I was about ten years old, break dancing was the in-thing. Kids sported black spiked belts, leather wrist bands, Jheri curls, and headbands. Of course, my mother had to find a me a stylish, different-looking belt. She found one that had handcuffs as a belt buckle. It actually came with keys. I decided to tease one of the girls at school, Sarah.

"I bet you won't let me put these handcuffs on you?" I teased.

Eventually she agreed to let me put them on her. Of course I had to show off, so when she asked me to take them off, I refused. We were in a small courtyard at Harry F. Abate Elementary School where we played during recess. Sarah had on the handcuffs when a teacher yelled, "Line up! Boys over here and girls over here," she said pointing to two different areas. "Follow me to the auditorium."

I can't remember why we had to go to the auditorium that day, but I remember leaving the handcuffs on Sarah until finally, a teacher spotted her. Sarah was just about to sit down. I was in the row behind her. The teacher yelled, "Come here, Sarah. Who handcuffed you?"

Sarah paused as if she didn't want to snitch. The teacher gestured to the Principal, Mr. Johnson, who was about twenty feet away near the stage. He was an older white man who never smiled. He had a big stomach and a reddish beard that came to a point because he always stroked it as he stared into our eyes.

"Why do you have handcuffs on, young lady?" Mr. Johnson asked Sarah.

She turned, looked at me, and then pointed, "Jaz put them on me."

Mr. Johnson looked over at me, stroked his beard and said, very loudly, "Let's go, Mr. Benson." I was suspended for two days.

When I was about 13, BB guns became the in-thing where I lived. All my friends got rifle BB guns for Christmas; my mother got me a machine-pump BB gun. We lived in Jordan Gardens, an expansive, fenced-in, urban development that attracted large families with well-respected elders, but it also housed some of the toughest teenagers in "The Falls."

I wanted a BB gun simply because all my friends were getting them. A couple of weeks after Christmas, a large number of animals began showing up dead around the neighborhood: birds, squirrels, cats. My friends were hunting small animals. One afternoon I saw five police cars parked alongside the Unity Park Housing Development. A couple of police officers tossed BB guns in their trunks. Kids cried, begging to get their guns back. Parents screamed at the cops.

The officers didn't take my gun. Shooting animals wasn't my style. One of my friends named Kurtis dared me once to shoot a bird. I hesitated for a few minutes, and then pulled the trigger. The bird fell to the ground, bloody and still. That would be the first and last time I ever killed anything. Before I pulled the trigger, I felt as though the bird sensed he was in danger. He looked down at me as if he knew what I was going to do. After shooting him I realized other birds were staring at me. My thought was that the bird could have been someone's mother or father, maybe someone's child, and the only reason I shot it was to prove I wasn't scared to do it. I felt like one of those vicious thugs in the 'hood who killed for no reason other than the fact that someone dared him to do it.

Some of the kids were so angry their guns were taken that, led by Kurtis, they found other ways to torture small animals. The same day the guns were taken, Kurtis noticed a cat on the side of a building. He deceivingly walked up to the cat as if he was going to caress it.

He called, "Here, kitty, kitty."

The cat walked over to Kurtis. He picked it up quickly by its tail, twirled it around in the air, and then let it go flying over a roof.

The following year bombers became the in-thing. Bombers were heavy coats with checkered sleeves made of cloth and solid torsos made of leather; they also had massive hoods lined with white fake fur. Most people had the white-and-black or blue-and-black or red-and-black coats; my mother got me a pink-and-black one for Christmas! The coat was beautiful, but it was pink. Back then, unless you were a pimp, you got teased by your friends for wearing pink clothing. I didn't want to wear the coat to school, but my mother made me. Friends and relatives laughed and joked about my pink coat. Aunt Ellen led the taunts, although she actually helped my mother pick it out. Go figure. I had to cuss out a couple of people, but after a month or so the comments and giggles became less and less.

The truth was, since my mother couldn't afford to get us a lot of presents like most kids in our 'hood got at Christmas; she did what she could by getting us something different. To her, different was special.

My mother was 16 years old when she had me. She moved out of my grandparents' house when she was 15. She was courageous and loving to most people around her, at least until you pissed her off. Maybe for this reason, she was quick to let people stay with us. It seemed as if there was always someone living with us. Basically relatives, friends, and their children, anyone who was either evicted or just homeless was welcome in my mother's home until they were able to get back on their feet. She was quick to help a friend in need and would give her last piece of bread to a child, but she was cursed with a rage that could not be matched. Women feared her and men admired her beauty, though they were cautious because of her anger.

When I was young, my mother had a rule that I had to be in the house before nightfall. One day when I was seven, I was playing outside and not paying attention to the time. It was dark when I ran up the stairs and busted through the door of our small apartment. My mother had water boiling on the stove. I looked around for other ingredients, wondering what she was cooking. I looked to the left and noticed her watching the television in the living room. She looked upset. Thoughts ran through my mind. Did I do something earlier? Was I really late? And most of all, was she going to whip me? I stood near the door for a few seconds just staring at her. I thought to myself, It's not me she's mad at because she would have yelled at me by now, or at least sent me to my room. She jumped up and walked toward the cabinet over the kitchen sink and grabbed a bag of grits.

"Ma, are we eating grits tonight?" I asked.

"Don't worry about it. Go take a bath," she snapped.

As I walked into the bathroom I noticed the bathtub was already half full with toys in it. I enjoyed taking a bath with toys; I could stay in there for hours. Maybe that was her intention. Shortly after I got in the tub I heard my mother yelling. I don't remember all the words but I know it had to do with Tommy, my brother's father, who had just come in and something about another woman, and then I heard a scream of pain. The bathroom door sprang open and Tommy rushed to the mirror. Smoke was coming from his shirt which he ripped off quickly. His chest was red and looked deformed. I realized my mother had thrown the scorching hot water and grits on him. Eventually he stopped crying and screaming and just stared into the mirror. I continued to play with my toys as if this was a normal situation. I didn't feel too sorry for Tommy; I was more excited it wasn't me she was mad at. Tommy glanced over his shoulder and said, "Your mother is crazy. I'm out of here."

He exited the bathroom and seconds later I heard the front door slam and footsteps running down the stairs. After I got out the tub I found my mother on the couch, motionless, watching the television again. I crept past her, put on my clothes, and went to bed. For some reason Tommy didn't call the police that night. He appeared a few months later as if nothing had happened.

This wasn't the last time my mother inflicted pain on a boyfriend. Jamil was my brother Rod's father. Rod is the youngest of my mother's four children. When I was around fifteen, my grandfather told me how my mother had stabbed Jamil seven times. We continued having a conversation about my mother's rage and how it affected me. He explained that she had left Jamil drowning in his own blood because she found a woman's phone number in his jeans. When she had confronted him about it, he responded with anger, accusing her of going through his private belongings. After a few minutes of screaming at each other, Jamil punched my mother in the eye, knocking her to the floor. She blindly walked into the kitchen, holding her face. Jamil followed her. She met him with a knife and repeatedly stabbed him in his chest and arms, then walked to my grandparents' place, sat down on the couch, and told my grandfather, "I tried to kill Jamil. I hope he dies."

"You don't want a body on your conscience and you don't want to live in prison away from your kids," my grandfather told her.

Mama agreed. She called 911 and told them that a man was bleeding to death in her apartment. Surprisingly, Jamil did not tell the police that my mother was the attacker. Instead he told them that someone had broken into her apartment and attacked him. He was hospitalized for a couple of days and then released with a few dozen stitches.

My father was the rare one who didn't fight with her that much, at least not physically. He left our home when I was about two years old. He left Niagara Falls and joined the Marines when I was three. The only time he returned was to visit. My mother became a single parent at the age of eighteen.

CHAPTER 3

BEING A MAN AT FOURTEEN

When I was about fourteen years old, my mother started disappearing on a regular basis. Sometimes I enjoyed it because it was an opportunity to stay with my grandparents, although my mother and my grandmother did not get along. My grandmother was one of the few people who stood up to my mother. My grandparents did not like how my mother beat me. My grandmother was quick to run to my rescue if I could find a way to sneak and call her. She was the rare person in my life who was patient with me, even though at times I abused her patience. I recall bursting into tantrums, kicking things, screaming at the top of my lungs, and crying as if someone was killing me when I couldn't get my way. Most of the time my grandparents just patiently waited for me to stop crying and once I did, they tenderly lectured me with love and affection.

My mother generally asked one or two of her best friends to watch us while she went out. Sometimes she wouldn't come back for two to four days. I didn't like staying with her friends, despite the fact that they both had kids around my age. Their places were so disgusting that I starved myself whenever I was left with them. Both homes had a horrific stench that always ruined my appetite. I could never figure out where the smell came from, but figured it could have had something to do with the old piss-stained mattresses in their home. The kitchen floors had a thick, brown film on them that made it hard to tell what color the tile was. The counters were littered with old cans, dirty dishes, and roaches that seemed to be having a ball. I didn't like touching anything. When they put food on the table, I sneaked and put mine in the garbage or fed it to the dog. Once in a while they caught me refusing to eat which would start a never-ending argument.

My mother's friend Rachelle had an especially loud and disgusting odor coming from her apartment. You could smell it about five feet from her front door. I wouldn't eat at all while I stayed there. I was, however, smart enough to now and again force a small piece of bread down my throat to keep up my energy. I was picky about what I ate and where I ate. I would only eat the food at my grandparents' house, my cousin's house, and at my own home. So after a couple days of my mother's disappearance, I usually found a way to call reinforcements, my grandparents, even though before my mother left she would always threatened to beat me if I called them. My grandfather normally found a way to bring me food without anyone knowing. I'd meet him at the corner and he'd give me an egg sandwich, Vienna sausages, an orange soda, and some type of candy in a brown-paper bag. He also brought enough candy for my brother and my sister, but they didn't need as much food as me, because they ate all the meals Rachelle provided for them. I also didn't sleep well at Rachelle's house. Her son was about two years younger than me. His mattresses was terribly stained and smelled like urine. The rug in his room was discolored from age and cluttered with broken toys. I normally fell asleep on the edge of the bed with my back up against the wall.

My grandmother's style was different. She didn't care to sneak me anything. When she found out that my mother had disappeared again, she was on Rachelle's front doorstep demanding that she allow us to go home with her. Rachelle put up a small fight since she knew my mother wouldn't approve, but it didn't take long for her to give in because generally, by that time, she was tired of us and fed up with my mother's disappearing acts.

About a year later, at age fifteen, I became the babysitter whenever my mother disappeared. She continued to periodically vanish for a couple of days at a time. Rumor was she was hanging out in Buffalo with a guy she liked. Meanwhile I spent a lot of days and nights raising my sister and my two brothers. My mother left my siblings with me so often that it was rare for me to have time to do anything else, like hang out with my friends.

I had little tolerance, if any, with my siblings, especially with my sister Kathika who is five years younger than me. My sister was like a news reporter. She told everything we did wrong, never what we did right. No matter how long my mother was gone, my sister would wait for her return and then broadcast everything. Most of the time, I just wanted to be left alone to watch TV. When interrupted, I screamed with rage, the scare tactic I used to make my siblings leave me alone. I didn't scream at my youngest brother Rod that much because he was so innocent and tried to stay out of my way. Rod, a.k.a. Pup, was three years old, quiet, and seemed to really miss Ma when she left.

My mother knew that Kathika would tell her everything I did and said. Like an elephant, Kathika's memory was flawless. "Thika", as we called her, was beautiful. She was light-skinned like my mother with long, beautiful hair and a smile that lit up the room, although she could also give you that evil look just like my mother. When she stared at me with her beady eyes I knew I was in trouble. Thika had a habit of walking into the living room, glimpsing up at me mischievously, walking Of course I got highly upset every time she did this; sometimes I just screamed and she just ignored me. Other times I would scream, grab her by the arm, and pull her into another room. She eventually returned, acting fearless and not bothered by my outbursts.

My other brother, Tommy, whom we called "Buddha," wasn't the telling type. Four years younger than Thika, he usually minded his own business, but if you crossed him, he responded like a violent Rottweiler. He could be calm like Pup, but vicious like me.

My brother Pup did no wrong. He was harmless, and he is still the most laidback of us all. When I was babysitting, he just watched TV or played with his toys. We barely had food to eat, but there were a couple of items that we could always depend on. One was the long block of "welfare cheese" that came in a brown, rectangular, cardboard box. I made macaroni and cheese, grilled cheese sandwiches, cheesy fries, cheesy eggs, and other concoctions with that block of cheese. The second item was Oodles of Noodles which had a powdered soup packet made of nothing but sodium. It came in a square-shaped, colorful, plastic pouch. If by chance we ran out, I could easily find a nickel to buy a pack at the store. We also kept milk, eggs, bread, Kool-Aid, frozen French fries, Jiffy cornbread, and hot dogs. This was what we ate and what most of the people I knew ate also—at least if they were poor like us. Of course, I was too young to be concerned about my health. I just wanted to feed the hunger. As I grew older, I began to understand that African-Americans' poor diets were probably why so many of us have high blood pressure, high cholesterol, diabetes, and other diseases affiliated with unhealthy eating.

These situations caused me to become creative. We normally didn't have food items that complemented one another, or the products we needed to prepare recipes. We didn't always have bread for hot dogs, sugar for Kool-Aid, milk for cereal, eggs for cornbread, or grease to fry French fries. At times we ate our cereal with water and our hot dogs with Oodles of Noodles instead of bread.

The best part was learning to fix French fries in the oven. Everyone ate whatever I fixed, especially Buddha, who made sure there were never leftovers.

Thika was the only one who relentlessly tested me. If I got out of hand, she said those magic words, "I'm telling!" Sometimes I tried to bribe her by offering her fifty cents to not tell something, but even that didn't appease her for long. Sooner or later she would demand more money or threaten again to tell whatever story she was spinning that day. Eventually, after I ran out of things to give her, she told Mother the secret she was just waiting to spill and my mother either whipped me or punished me by not allowing me to go outside or watch TV. Each time my mother left, I took my frustrations out on my siblings because I was forced to watch out for my siblings, had no freedom of my own, and couldn't hang out with my friends. I certainly couldn't take my anger out on my mother; I couldn't even question her when she returned. So while I babysat I just wanted to be left alone.

Our life was up and down, a roller coaster of emotions. We hated it whenever my mother disappeared, but we always had the first of the month to look forward to. That was payday for people on welfare and Ma always got us something special, like a shirt, a game, or some magnificent food like pizza and chicken wings. On the first we looked forward to hearing the doorbell ring. I usually ran the fastest, so I was the one who greeted the delivery man. He would be standing there with his arms full of food, most often a party tray of pizza and 50 wings. In retrospect, I think this was my mother's way of saying she was sorry. Even now, I love myself some great chicken wings and pizza.

CHAPTER 4

THE LAW IN THE 'HOOD

Like most people in the 'hood, we had a small black-and-white television that sat on a large television that didn't work. I used to love to watch cartoons like Popeye and Tom and Jerry. When I was about six years old, I was at home watching TV and I heard yelling coming from outside.

It was a woman's voice. My mother heard it too. She ran to the window, paused for a moment, and then ran out the front door. As soon as she was out of sight, I ran to the window and looked out. A woman was brutally beating a child. I watched as my mother grabbed the woman and pushed her away from the child. The woman retaliated and attacked my mother. My mother threw a punch and the woman fell to the ground. She jumped on the woman and continued to punch her. It was as if my mother was possessed by something evil. I heard sirens from a distance. Finally the noise from the police cars seemed to awaken my mother from her trance. She stopped hitting the woman and stood up. The woman's face was bleeding and she lay on the ground lifeless.

By the time the police pulled up, other people had come out of their apartments to witness the mayhem. After about five minutes, one of the policeman grabbed my mother by the arm and escorted her to his car. I remember her looking up towards the window, it was as if she looked right into my eyes as if she was trying to apologize without using her mouth. I couldn't help replaying the scene of her beating the woman, her aggressiveness, and the steely, fearless look on her face. I found that I admired what I had seen, and from that day on, my mother's way of fighting became my way of fighting.

Some time later, I heard someone coming up the stairs. The front door opened. It was my mother. "Go to bed, Jaz," she demanded. As I unhurriedly walked toward my room, I looked back at my mother.

She was hurting, but not physically. She was staring at the floor, leaning against the wall between the kitchen and the living room. I had never seen her like this.

"Are you alright?" I asked. She didn't respond.

"Good night," I said.

Not too long afterward I heard her crying in her bedroom. This wasn't like her. The mother I knew was tough and fearless. A couple of weeks later I got in to trouble for fighting. Along with my whippin' I was grounded from playing with my toys. I had just received this very cool racetrack. My mother had me disassemble it and put it back into the box and give it to her. She walked the box across our small living room and put it on the top shelf in the closet. Shortly after that I saw my mother sitting on the porch of our apartment duplex talking to a friend. I had just gotten home from school. I ran up to her and gave her a big hug. She wrapped her arms around me and told me there was food on the stove.

I yelled for my sister when I got to the top of the stairs. "Let's eat, Thika!" No one replied. It was obvious I was home alone. I looked out the window to see if my mother was still outside talking to her friend and she was. I ran over to the closet in the living room to grab my racetrack, soon realizing that I was too small to reach it. I quickly grabbed a chair from the kitchen and pulled it over to the closet. I climbed up on the chair and immediately noticed a box of bottles that were full of a bright pink syrup sitting next to my race car set. It looked like medicine. I grabbed one of the bottles, and when I did, I heard a crackling sound come from the steps leading to our apartment. The duplex we lived in was old. You couldn't sneak up those stairs if you wanted to.

My mother is coming! I thought, swiftly putting the mysterious pink bottle back in place. I rushed to try to get the chair over to the kitchen table, but it was clear that I wasn't going to make it! Suddenly the door opened. I stood trembling, caught–trying to return the chair, which was still about six feet from the table. I looked at the door-and saw that it was my sister.

"What you doing?" Thika asked in her soft, infantile voice. Before I could answer, she looked at the chair in my hand and continued, "Ooooohhh, I'm telling Ma."

My sister was spoiled and good at telling on me even when she didn't know what she was telling. Because of this, I was obsessed with getting her in trouble. My mother would never whip Thika. If my sister was caught doing something, somehow the situation became my fault. "You should have been watching her" was my mother's number one line.

For instance, one day while babysitting my sister and her friend Vickie, I noticed a lot of hair in a small, dark-blue garbage can in Thika's room. Instantly I ran into the living room where Vickie and Thika sat on the floor innocently playing with their baby dolls. As I ran up to them Thika looked up at me with her mouth open as if she had already guessed what I was about to say.

"What did you do?" I asked. Thika pointed at Vickie and said, "Vickie cut her hair."

"She cut hers too," Vickie quipped.

I bent over to take a closer look at Thika's hair. I noticed that she was missing a small piece of her hair on the left side of her head. Next, I looked at Vickie's hair and found she was missing a lot of hair in the back.

"You two were playing with scissors and you cut your hair? I'm telling!" I screamed.

Vickie started to cry, but Thika continued to play with her dolls. Anxiously I watched the clock, waiting for my mother to come home. A couple of hours later I heard someone coming up the stairs. I ran to the door and opened it. It was my mother and Vickie's mother Rhonda.

"I should whip you," my mother said before she even walked inside the apartment. "You know better. Don't ever open this door without asking who it is."

"Ma, Thika and Vickie cut their hair," I said.

My mother paused, gawked at me and asked, "What do you mean they cut their hair?"

Rhonda, who looked like she was high on some type of drug, immediately started walking aggressively through the apartment, looking for her daughter. She didn't say a word, she just lethargically walked from room to room. She had on a pair of thick glasses, a small afro, and a look in her eyes that reflected a woman who didn't know where she was, although she had been in our apartment several times. Instead of going to the right, where my sister's room was, she headed to the left through the living room and toward my room.

My mother watched Rhonda. "Rhonda, Thika's bedroom is back here," she said, pointing in the right direction. Again, without saying a word Rhonda followed my mother to Thika's bedroom. I walked into the living room, sat on the couch, and smiled. My sister is finally going to get in trouble, I thought to myself.

Then I heard a series of screams. It wasn't coming from my sister; it was coming from Vickie. I jumped off the couch and ran toward my sister's room. I peeked around the corner and witnessed Rhonda violently hitting Vickie with a belt. I mean she was hitting her with everything she had, again and again. She hit Vickie for at least three to five minutes off and on, only pausing for a few seconds in-between hits. My mother was sitting at the kitchen table crying.

"Ma, what's wrong?" I asked. She didn't respond.

Rhonda was screaming as she whipped her daughter, "I can't believe you did this to your hair! How could you? Why? I'm going to beat your ass!"

At first I didn't understand why Rhonda was so upset until my mother finally said, crying, "Why did Thika cut her long and beautiful hair? I can't believe she cut her long and beautiful hair."

What I came to realize is that Thika and Vickie's long hair meant a lot to women like my mother and Rhonda. My mother didn't believe in putting chemicals, such as perms and relaxers, in a young girl's hair. She only used a hot comb to straighten Thika's hair. I surmised they had a longstanding connection to the rituals that involved caring for their daughters' long hair and that they took pride in the treasured results.

As my mother sat there crying she suddenly looked up at me and said, "I should beat your ass! You let Thika cut her hair. Where the hell were you? You were supposed to be watching them. How could you let them play with scissors?"

My heart raced. I was used to getting a whippin', but I had never gotten one while my mother was in this state of mind. My mother stood up and walked toward me. I backed up in the direction of my sister's bedroom. Thika was balled up on her bed watching her friend getting a beating. I continued to back up until I passed Thika's room. My mother stopped at the doorway and gazed at the scene inside.

"Rhonda, stop! You're going to kill her!" my mother screamed, grabbing Rhonda and guiding her to the kitchen. They stood there, holding each other and crying together. I went and stood at my sister's bedroom door. Thika was just sitting there as if she was watching TV. Moments later my mother came around the corner with the belt Rhonda had used. She walked into my sister's room and struck Thika once with the belt.

"Don't you leave this room tonight!" she said.

I couldn't believe my mother only hit Thika once. Then she walked out of the bedroom, looked at me and swung the belt in my direction.

She missed, but she screamed, "Go to your room, Shondell, and don't come out! You should have been watching her!" I knew if she called me Shondell, which is my middle name, she was really upset with me. I ran through the kitchen and the living room and into my room Fifteen years would pass before the pink bottles on the top shelf of the closet surfaced again. I was working for a computer company that was contracted by the local Board of Education. I didn't know too much about computers, but my mother had advised me that I needed to get a job in computers if I was going to be successful. During the interview process, the interviewer recognized that I didn't really know a lot about computers, but he hired me anyway because he said he liked my ambition.

One day while I was working, a teacher's assistant approached me with a frown on her face. "What is your name?" she asked.

"Jaz," I replied.

"What is your real name?"

"Jaz."

"Jaz what?"

"Jaz Benson."

"What is your mother's last name?"

"Camp," I said.

Her face turned a ghostly white. "I thought you looked familiar. Your mother is Linda Camp. She's the reason why I'm no longer with my husband Detective Counts," she offered out the blue.

"Why is that?" I asked.

The woman began to cry. I wasn't sure what to think, but I figured it had to be bad. I knew my mother had used drugs and she'd lived through a lot of other troubles, but I didn't know all of the details of her life. For instance, currently I'm not clear about what drugs she used. I guess I have never really wanted to face the truth. Most of my friends knew more about my mother's life than I did. They were aware of her drug use, but they were afraid to talk to me about it. My mind ran through a number of the possibilities as the woman cried for a minute or so without saying a word, then she said something that changed my life.

"I divorced my husband, because of what he did to your mother and a few other people. Years ago, when you were young, your mother got into a fight with a woman who was beating up a child in your neighborhood. My husband at that time, Detective Counts, was the first person on the scene. He put your mother in his police car and offered an 'alternative' to going to jail. He threatened that he could put her in jail for a long time or she could avoid jail by selling drugs for him. He figured she would agree since she didn't want to risk losing her kids. She started selling cough syrup for him and then sold other drugs. My husband stole drugs from drug dealers to redistribute them and passed the drugs along to people like your mother who didn't have a choice. Eventually your mother started using some of the drugs. She was the perfect bait for him in view of how well known and respected she was in the 'hood."

Prior to this I didn't know why my mother had started using drugs, and I never thought to even ask. After hearing the woman's account of what happened to my mother, the first thing that came to my mind was that it wasn't her fault. I felt compassion for her. It was entrapment. She was confronted with a choice, that either way would have led her down a dark road. Yes, my mother could have avoided protecting the child that day. She could have controlled her rage but she didn't and was a changed woman after that fight. As time went on she grew more bitter and exasperated with life. Now that I recognized her dilemma, I could see clearly that this one incident had taken the wind out of her. I thought it was the fight and being arrested that changed her, but now I understood that for a strong black woman who once stood up for those weaker than herself, to have given in to a life of drugs and destruction was devastating.

Later in life the drugs she used began to take over her identity. She became labeled as a drug addict, but still she wasn't like most addicts in the 'hood. When she wasn't high, she was still trying to rescue kids from abused homes. Even though I never wanted to admit it, or face it, I heard she was using crack. Crackheads, as they were called, were like zombies willing to do anything, including steal from family to purchase more crack. My mother, at least as far as I know, did not steal from family, although I heard she stole small items from department stores and exchanged them for crack.

There were a few apartment buildings in the 'hood where crackheads were known to hang out. My mother didn't normally hang out in the open when she was high. She gathered with other addicts in those rodent-infested apartment buildings. The closest I ever came to witnessing my mother high was talking to her over the phone. I could tell she was high because she slurred her speech when she spoke. I knew it was unsafe for most crackheads in the streets. If the drug dealers weren't abusing them, they would sooner or later get arrested for either using drugs or stealing. Drug dealers beat addicts just because they got on their nerves. Other times they raped the female addicts and killed the ones who stole from drug dealers to buy drugs from another dealer.

Even with this being known, people around our community still held respect for my mother, which was unusual. It could have been because she still expressed a great deal of compassion for her community or, some say my mother got respect because she had a very protective and vengeful son—namely, me.

The 'hood inspires toughness…it has a darkness about it that promotes craziness. A guy name Kurtis was one of the toughest guys I was acquainted with. He might have also been the craziest. He had an indescribable darkness about him. I fought to protect my family, friends, and myself, but Kurtis sometimes fought for the fun of it. I don't know how or what made him so fearless, but he was, and he was famous for it. He'd jump pizza deliverymen and ambush innocent bystanders walking down the street. It didn't matter to him. He was vicious. I think what scared me the most about Kurtis was that he was tougher than I am.

During the winter months, when the grounds were covered with ice, Kurtis created an unconventional way to move about. He strategically waited for a driver to get in a car and then he approached the car, stooped down out of sight of the rearview mirrors, and grabbed a hold of the back bumper. He held on real tight, squatted down, and let the car pull him from block to block on the ice with nothing, but his sneakers on. I did this a couple of times, but it wasn't for me. I was courageous when it came to fighting, but I feared putting my life on the line for other stupid things.

We had this little clique (some might call us a gang) in which I was the peculiar one. I didn't mind a good fight, but again, I didn't like to fight just to hurt people so a lot of times when the clique roamed around hurting people I went home. Unity Park was directly across the street from Jordan Gardens. Kurtis and some of our other friends used to order pizza for random addresses. When the delivery man entered the hallway, they beat him and took his money—and the pizza Kurtis was the ring leader. He was the reason why restaurants wouldn't deliver pizza to Unity Park or in Jordan Gardens where I lived for a few years.

I went with Kurtis a couple of times to fight other rival 'hoods like Center Court. We all met in the middle of the street with bats and sticks and fought until the cops came to break us up. Kurtis was the first to swing a bat and the last to leave. I kept a good social distance from Kurtis so our paths didn't cross often. I was just as tough as he was and we both were very much aware of the consequence of crossing each other.

One day, I saw Kurtis and my cousin Anthony walking across the field in Unity Park one day. I ran up to Anthony. He seemed startled. "Jaz, I just helped them beat up a man for no reason," he said. "Kurtis pointed at a white man walking and just told me to hit him and I did, then Kurtis and the others came over to help. They kicked and punched this guy until he couldn't move." I looked over at Kurtis and glared right into his eyes. He smiled at me. I felt something bad was about to happen. I was known for protecting Anthony. Kurtis quickly intercepted, "Anthony has one more test. He has to fight Phats," he said.

Phats, the baby-faced youngest of our group was a little overweight, but not really fat. He was standing near Kurtis when Kurtis ordered him to fight. Phats put up his fist and got into position to fight Anthony. They were close friends up to this point and their mothers were close friends too. Anthony wasn't scared of Phats, but he feared the end result: what Kurtis would do next if he beat Phats. They both shot a couple of punches at each other and then I broke them up. "Get out of here, Anthony. I got this," I shouted. Anthony gradually walked away. I started beating on Phats. While I was on top of him someone began kicking me. I held Phats down so he couldn't go anywhere, but I was also protecting my face. My elbows were on Phats's face, but my forearms were covering my face. There was more than one person kicking me. Then all of a sudden it stopped. In pain, I gradually got to my feet. To the left I saw Ernie, another friend, walking away with his head down. I guessed something was happening that he didn't want to have anything to do with.

To the right I saw Kurtis and Shock chasing Anthony across the field. I took off after them while Phats lay unconscious on the ground. Anthony was running toward his apartment. As I got closer, I saw them run into Anthony's place. I followed and got to the apartment door just as they were attacking Anthony in the living room. He was on the couch on his back swinging punches while both Shock and Kurtis swung at him. As much as I wanted to help, I hesitated to walk into the living room, because Anthony's mother didn't allow us in there. It was a room with old family pictures, two couches covered with plastic, and beautiful old lamps without bulbs. The rug didn't have a stain, the light-green couch looked untouched, and the oak dining-room table always seemed to shine. I grabbed Shock and tried to push him out of the room. I was getting nowhere when I heard a scream. It was my Aunt Ernestine. She was running down the stairs.

"What the hell is going on?!" she yelled as she got closer. Kurtis and Shock took off running past her as she came around the corner. She had no idea what was going on, but she immediately suspected I was the culprit for all the noise. You're always in trouble, Jaz! Get out!" she hollered.

The next day at school, I passed Kurtis in the hall and he quickly turned around and said. "What's up, Jaz? Do you want to skip fourth period with us?" He spoke as if nothing had happened. I paused for a moment and then just walked away. I had a lot of respect for Kurtis, because he was so tough and he didn't seem to be scared of anything, but I vowed to never hang out with him again. We stayed friends from a distance. Funny thing was, Anthony continued to hang out with him.

Eventually Kurtis told me what my mother was doing. I stopped trying to ignore her behavior and just accepted who she was. The teacher's assistant's disclosure allowed me to release my own judgment of my mother. Now my mom spends every day giving to others; it seemed a natural progression of her journey. She will walk miles to feed an elder, patiently French braid a young girl's hair in the neighborhood, or care for the babies in the family.

She changed before I did, and at the time some people who knew us would have said she left an unmatchable rage in her son, but actually watching her change her life taught me that I could change mine. She did the best she could after being abandoned by the men in her life. She raised three boys and one girl alone. My father moved miles away from us to the South. My sister's father, Johnny, died when she was about 7 years old; he was shot while gambling during a card game. One brother's father became an alcoholic, and the other went to prison.

CHAPTER 5

THE SEXUAL ABUSE

Before I came along, my mother treated Ellen, my mother's sister and therefore my aunt, as if she were her daughter. Although Ellen had both of her parents to go to, she always ran to my mother for comfort. She was also very spoiled by my grandfather. She was one of the only females in the 'hood who owned close to 100 pairs of shoes. She did no wrong in my grandfather's eyes. My grandfather spoiled me as well, but he would turn his back on me when it came to Ellen. My Aunt Ellen played a huge role in my life in regard to me becoming a man who loves books and owns a bookstore. Later in life, starved for happiness and positive energy, my success was due to some of the pain Ellen branded me with. It's the rebel in me!

It started when I was a baby and Aunt Ellen was left to babysit me. My mother was shocked when she came home and heard me screaming. She flew up the stairs to find Ellen reading a book as she sat next to the bedroom door, calmly thrusting the door back and forth. On the other side of the door was my crib, which was being banged each time Ellen pushed the door. On another occasion, while babysitting me, my mother caught Ellen pouring salt down my throat. Sometimes she would attack me violently when no one else was around. I felt trapped, because if I told on her, my grandfather would yell at me, **and if I didn't say anything, Ellen would torture me even more**. There was one person who suspected that something wasn't right about Ellen, and that was her mother, my grandma.

In spite of the questionable incidents, my mother continued to let Ellen babysit me and my sister, even after Ellen vowed not to try and kill me anymore. I suppose she kept her word, because we didn't die from being in her care, but she wounded us deeply in a way that at times left me feeling dead.

I remember when I was about 10 years old, my mother left Ellen to watch Anthony, his sister, Trina, and me. Ellen was about sixteen at the time. Not long after my mother exited Ellen told us, "Get ready, because we are going to take pictures." The three of us were excited and went into my room to play dress-up. We hadn't been in there long before Ellen told us we didn't need to get dressed up.

"We're taking pictures with our clothes off," she said.

We all looked at each other. Even at our age we were intuitive enough to know this was a strange request and that something about it was just plain wrong, but Ellen had a distinctive authority over us. She was a bully with a strange hypnotizing stare that frightened us and made us obey. I don't remember why, but my sister wasn't around. In retrospect I wish she had been there, because Ellen didn't have any influence over Thika. My sister would have refused to obey orders and then she would have told our mother.

"Take off your clothes!" Ellen demanded, glaring into each of our eyes with firmness. She then requested that we pose in certain positions. She made me and Trina hug each other and then lay on top of each other. I was uncomfortable, and I felt it was wrong, but I went along with it as if we were just playing house. I couldn't help but feel sorry for Anthony as he cried throughout the whole ordeal. His sister Trina was only a year younger than Ellen, but like the rest of us, she obeyed Ellen's demands out of fear. My brother was in another room asleep.

Ellen didn't even have a real camera. She acted like she was holding a camera and taking pictures by looking through a circle she made with her hands. At times she stood at the doorway and pretended to take pictures while we posed nude. She then had the three of us jump up and down on the top bunk bed with our heads brushing the ceiling as we bounced up and down in the air.

A bunch of my cousins, including Anthony, Trina, Brenda, and Kesha, at times stayed at my grandparents' house for the weekend. When my grandmother worked the overnight shift she left Ellen in charge while she took a nap during the day. My grandfather hung out at the bar up the street with his friends most of the day so we were left alone under Ellen's supervision. Sometimes, right there in our grandparents' house, she had us pose nude again. In some cases she ordered us to touch each other.

A couple of times I told on Ellen. My grandmother would get upset and order Ellen to tell the truth, but Ellen would just deny all of the accusations. Granddad didn't want to accept that his princess was really a witch, but Grandma was on to her. On the one hand, Grandma loved it when her grandchildren stayed at her home, but on the other hand, she had to worry about what Ellen would do next. One time I called Grandma when Ellen asked us to take off our clothes. Grandma was asleep in a room down the hallway. Moments later she banged on the locked door to Ellen's room. I ran to open it. Grandma looked over at Ellen and said, "What's going on in here?"

"They're all playing house with no clothes on," Ellen said. "I told them to keep their clothes on, but they wouldn't listen."

Grandma didn't believe her because by now we were all accusing Ellen of wrongdoings. She told Ellen she was grounded for a month and lectured the rest of us about listening to Ellen. Later that day, Grandma made us egg sandwiches. Egg sandwiches were a favorite around my grandmother's house. There was something about the way she made them, and though they are simple to make, I can't duplicate the way my grandma made them! While exiting the dining room Grandma turned and said, "Eat your sandwich and then you can play with your toys, except for you, Ellen. You go straight to bed after you're done. I'm going back to sleep."

Ellen was sitting next to me. Soon as she heard Grandma make it to the top of the stairs, she leaned over my plate and spit on my sandwich. She whispered in my ear, "I'm telling your mother you asked everyone to take off their clothes."

I got a whippin' the following day because of what Ellen told my mother. The nude sessions with Ellen continued sporadically throughout the next couple of years. She was smart enough not to demand it every time we were left alone. At times she would have us touch each other. I felt humiliated, not only because of what we were doing, but because I let Ellen tell me what to do. I couldn't stand that I was afraid of her.

After a while we all became numb to the situation. At first, Anthony and some of the other cousins cried. By this point, no one cried. We just all played along until Ellen gave the okay to put our clothes back on. Funny though, it seemed when it was obvious that we were no longer bothered by her ordeal she stopped asking us to take off our clothes.

Grandma told me after our grandfather died that Ellen would soon be punished for how she mistreated people. My grandfather died of cancer. He died when I was about 24 years old. He was a treasure in our family, but he had one weakness: he gave Ellen anything she asked for and he protected her no matter how much wrong she did. The family had so much respect for Granddad that, for the most part, we were all hesitant to speak of the wrong things that Ellen did. Granddad was known for helping the family financially. He gave all the grandchildren a dollar every time we saw him and every so often he helped his kids when they had trouble with bills and food. Keep in mind, my grandparents lived in the ghetto, too, but they didn't believe in saving money, instead, they would help family members with any extra income they had. Again, Ellen was his favorite. He got upset even when his wife said something bad about Ellen.

Grandma said Ellen's kids would be the ones who would pay her back for all the wrong she had done, especially to children. My grandmother told me this at least 30 times even after she was diagnosed with Alzheimer's. I guess this sentiment was so deeply embedded in her memory and Grandma was right. As adults, Ellen's three daughters drive her nuts! The oldest one is always trying to hustle people out of their money. She had a scheme going where she answered ads for couples who wanted to have a child but couldn't. Once the couple gave her the first payment to be a surrogate, she lied about being pregnant and then disappeared. Ellen's other daughter dates a well-known drug dealer, smokes marijuana a lot, and has a kid that she doesn't want. At present, the youngest child only asks for money all the time.

I didn't have a lot of luck with babysitters. When I was about 7 years old I was laying in my racing car bed, almost asleep, when the babysitter entered my room and asked if she could lie next to me. She was a friend of my mother's that lived in the neighborhood. Although I didn't see her often she babysat us a couple of times. I didn't care, but since my bed was small, she had to lie on top of me.

"Can I touch you?" she asked. I remember falling asleep while she played with my penis. Unfortunately, molestation seemed to be a part of life in my neighborhood. Maybe it was because so many of the children were left alone without supervision. We were easy prey for the adults who were suffering from all kinds of mental issues.

Around the same time that this babysitter asked to play with my penis, this guy named Daryl made another proposal. Daryl was living a couple of houses down from me. He had to be about seventeen years old. Anthony and I did everything in our power to avoid him, but sometimes Daryl hunted us down. He forced us to follow him to his backyard. Next we had to follow him through a big hole that led under his porch. Only a little light shone under the porch. Mostly it was nothing but small dirt hills and old car parts under the gloomy porch. It was just three feet high, so we had to crawl.

Daryl had his sister follow us into the pit as well. She was about my age. His exact words were: "I'll let you sleep with my sister if you let me put my penis in your behind." Of course we said no, so then it escalated from an invite to a demand. He forced us to pull down our pants and bend over. I remember wanting to cry, but couldn't. After he finished he made us have sex with his sister. Neither one of us really wanted too. We weren't attracted to her at all, but he made it sound like he was doing us a favor.

One day after school I watched Daryl escort a young female onto the bus. I recognized her from our neighborhood. She looked upset, nervous, and scared. Daryl made her sit next to him in the back of the bus. I sat a couple of seats in front of them. A few minutes into the ride, I looked back and saw her head hanging from the edge of the dark green, torn seat. Her long black hair hung almost touching the floor. She was lying on her back. She had a beautiful skin tone, but I couldn't tell if she was white, Hispanic, or Indian. She looked stunned, but had a dejected look on her face as tears fell to the floor creating a small puddle on the black surface. Her head was wobbling a lot and it wasn't from the bus. When the bus finally came to my stop, I quickly ran to the back of the bus. Daryl looked up at me, jumped up, and pulled up his pants.

"Get out of here, Jaz, before you get hurt!" he yelled.

I felt sorry for the girl. This was my first eye-opener in regards to what it looked like to be violated. I had to see it happen to someone I felt was truly innocent before I understood what it meant to be a victim. Even today I still find it hard to believe that he raped her in broad daylight, on a school bus, and no one said anything, including me. I think as a young boy in the 'hood I thought my life was normal, that all kids lived this way. Most of this kind of sexual horror in my life occurred between 6 and 10 years old, yet the code in the 'hood was, no matter what, you don't tell. I didn't say anything about the sexual abuse until I was 31 years old. I was not only scared to tell anyone, but I was embarrassed as well.

CHAPTER 6

BECOMING A FATHER

I was nineteen years old, it was about six o'clock in the evening, and I was working at a pizzeria when I saw the manager walking real fast toward me with an unusual look on her face. From about 50 feet away, she stared at me as she approached me. She always walked fast. I used to wonder whether she was trying to impress the boss or if she just liked walking that fast. She came up to me, caught her breath, and said, "Tiffany is at the hospital. I think your son is about to be born." Before I could respond, she continued, "You can leave. I'll have someone finish the dishes."

I ran to get my coat from the back room and then headed toward the front of the restaurant. As I rushed toward the exit, my cousin Anthony entered. Like the manager, he was walking fast toward me with an unusual look on his face.

"I know. I'm on my way to the hospital," I said.

He looked puzzled. "What?"

"My son is about to be born. That's why you're here, right?" I said excitedly.

"Jaz, Reggie is in town. He wants us to go to Buffalo with him. He's going to introduce us to Jodeci! This could be our big break," Anthony said. He went on to say that Reggie wanted us to meet the R&B music group Jodeci because they were looking for young acts to open for them. At this time, I wasn't too familiar with Jodeci, but I trusted Anthony. Unlike me, Anthony sat in front of the television every day and watched hours of videos.

Most young boys in the 'hood wanted to either be an athlete or a rapper. Since I wasn't good at basketball or football, I chose to be a rapper. I did a show with Anthony at a rugged club in The Falls called the Monte Carlo. Anthony was the singer and I was the rapper. That was my first time on stage.

The crowd loved us. I wasn't like most rappers; I had on a pair of dressy maroon slacks and a multi-colored collar shirt. This was odd during a time when most rappers wore saggy jeans and oversized T-shirts. A couple of people in the front row began yelling, "Go, Jazzy! Go, Jazzy!" and that's how I got the nickname Jaz. I stopped Anthony in the middle of his excitement.

"Give me a ride. I need to go by the hospital," I said.

Anthony looked concerned. He got like this when it came to music. Everything came secondary to the possibility of being noticed or getting a record deal for him. During the 15-minute ride to the hospital I was quiet. I was hoping Tiffany wasn't ready to give birth, which would give me a little time to run to Buffalo with Anthony.

At the hospital I was greeted by a couple of my family members in the waiting room. I approached the desk and asked where I could find Tiffany. I anxiously walked into the room. She was lying in a small bed near the window. My first words were, "Are you all right?"

"Does it look like I'm all right?" she said.

Right then a doctor entered the room and told us it would be about three hours before she had our son. I sat in a chair near her bed as she dozed off to sleep. So many thoughts were running through my head. How can I take care of a baby? I'm just a bus boy at a local pizzeria. I rationalized that the opportunity to meet Jodeci could increase my chances of getting into the music industry. I convinced myself that this might provide the means for me to become a good father. Buffalo was only a half hour away from The Falls. I figured I could make it back before she had our baby. I looked over at Tiffany and told her that I would be back.

Her voice was a whisper, "Where are you going?"

"I just have to make a quick run with Anthony. I'll be right back."

She looked up at me and slightly rolled her eyes, as if she felt I was about to do something stupid and wouldn't make it back before our baby was born. I kissed her on the forehead and quickly walked out the room.

Anthony was leaning against the wall in the waiting room with an apprehensive look on his face. I told him that I would run up to Buffalo with him, but we had to be quick. He called his mother from a nearby pay phone and asked if he could use her car a little longer.

We stopped by Reggie's place first. He had us listen to a song he was going to propose to Jodeci. He had written and produced the song and had, had a local group sing it. He was hopeful Jodeci would like the song and use it on their next album. They actually did use the song which is called *What About Us?* As I watched the clock, I couldn't help but think about the local group that sang the song for Reggie. I knew them all, including the lead singer named Vinnie, who was a good friend of mine. I guessed that Reggie had told him that this particular song was going to be their breakthrough hit when the truth was

Reggie simply wanted a track to sell to Jodeci. Reggie just needed some voices and a group that had a similar style to Jodeci.

We listened to Reggie and his song for a good while and then we followed him up to Buffalo. All I could think about was Tiffany having our baby. My head was still full of questions. Would I make it back in time? Will I be a good father? Will this trip be worth it? Is it fate? Will Jodeci help us get a record deal or was this me just being immature? Would anything come out of it besides me missing the birth of my child?

Finally we arrived at the Hyatt Regency Hotel. Reggie went into the parking ramp while we drove around looking for a free parking space on the street which was always a challenge in Buffalo. By the time we parked, Reggie was nowhere in sight.

"Let's just go back. We don't know what room they're staying in," I told Anthony.

"Are you serious? We didn't come all this way to just turn back!" he yelled.

Anthony was the risk taker. When it came to music he always found a way to convince me that something crazy was the right thing to do. I followed him into the hotel. We walked into the enormous hotel lobby and I instantly looked to Anthony.

"Now what?" I asked.

"Let's just get on the elevator and go to the top floor. That's normally where the 'big dogs' stay," he replied with confidence.

I was stunned by the elegance of the hotel. Up to this point I had never been in a hotel that nice. We reached the top floor and leisurely walked down the beautiful, carpeted hallway. Out of nowhere, a short, skinny black man ran out of one room and straight into the room directly across the hallway. He only had on a pair of dingy white underwear.

"I think that was K-Ci," Anthony said.

"Who is K-Ci?" I asked.

Anthony explained that he was the lead singer of Jodeci. This couldn't be right I thought–a star like K-Ci running around in dingy underwear?

Anthony ran up to the door the man ran into and knocked. A guy about my size and build opened the door. The guy who ran across the hallway was now sitting in a chair while Reggie cut his hair. There was another light-skinned man in deep thought gazing out the window. Later I found out his name was DeVante. Anthony and I sat at the edge of one of the double beds.

"You better get away from that window before you fall out again!" the man who opened the door yelled to DeVante.

That's when I realized that the guys were actually the members of the group Jodeci. The one who opened the door was Jo-Jo, the guy getting his haircut was K-Ci, and the one sitting near the window in deep thought was DeVante. Jo-Jo went on to tell us that DeVante had once fallen out a hotel window and broken most of the bones in his upper body.

When K-Ci was done getting his hair cut another guy came in from an open door that led to another room; his name was Mr. Dalvin. As Mr. Dalvin walked toward Reggie to get his hair cut he looked at us and asked no one in particular, "Who are these guys?"

Reggie answered with a grin on his face, "This is Jaz and Anthony. They got this little rap-and-sing thing going on."

Mr. Dalvin asked us about living in The Falls. Jo-Jo told us they had family in that part of the state. There was something about DeVante that intrigued me. He told us he was the producer of the group. I could tell he was the brains behind their sound and image. We had a brief conversation about a guy he said was going to rule the music industry.

"Why do you feel this man is going to be so great? Is he a good singer or rapper?" I asked. "Who is he?"

"He is neither a great singer nor rapper. He's smart," said DeVante. "We call him Puff Daddy."

DeVante was intrigued by Puff Daddy's ambition to be great at what he did. In that moment I decided I wanted to be great at what I did as well. Two hours into listening and observing, I realized that Jodeci wasn't going to make us superstars. Don't get me wrong, they were all down to earth and welcoming, but their hands were full with their own stardom. K-Ci was a little distant and didn't say much, but I could tell he was the attitude behind the bad boy image of the group. Jo-Jo, K-Ci's older brother, joked about K-Ci having a quick tongue that always got the group into trouble. Jo-Jo continued to give examples of how he had to pull K-Ci out of physical confrontations.

I was getting more and more restless, contemplating the possibility that I was going to miss my baby being born. I wanted to leave so badly, but I couldn't get up the nerve to just stand up and say "bye." I kept trying to get Anthony's attention by signaling with my hands, "Let's go," but he was engrossed in the moment. We had arrived at the hotel around 9 PM and it was now around 1 AM Finally everyone looked exhausted and ready to go to bed. All the way back to The Falls I thought about how angry people were going to be at me and how much of a bad person they would think I was for going to Buffalo.

Of course by the time we got back to the hospital my son had been born. I was hurt to the point that I felt like throwing up. My choice, which was a major mistake, caused me to miss the birth of my son. To this day Tiffany has never forgiven me for not being beside her that night and rightfully so. That one irresponsible decision spawned a hatred for me with Tiffany. She didn't have to hate me for not being there, I hated myself. Although I take full responsibility for not being there when my son was born, I still wish I'd had a dad at that time to teach and scold me about the choices I was making, one who could guide me to do better and make better choices. I was trying to be a father without having anyone to teach me how to be one.

Nevertheless, my son DeShaan saved me when he was born. I now had a reason to live; it was no longer just about me. DeShaan would teach me how to become a better man. If I didn't want him to take on my anger I had to change my attitude. I learned to change things about myself—one at a time — so I could encourage my son. I made even the simplest decisions while thinking of him. If I wanted DeShaan to be healthy I had to exercise more and eat better. Unlike parents who preached, "Do what I say, not what I do," I believed I had to lead by example.

CHAPTER 7

TRYING TO UNDERSTAND MY ANGER

When my son was about 4 years old, I recorded a song in the studio about him. I named it after him, "DeShaan." At the time my son lived with his mother a short fifteen minutes from the recording studio. Excited and impatient, I dashed out the studio to his mother's house. I had actually finished two songs that day. In addition to "DeShaan," I did a remix of the classic R&B song "Tender Love," originally recorded by the Force MDs. An Italian friend of mine, Joe, sung on the "Tender Love" track and he rode with me to pick up my son.

I pulled up in the driveway, hopped out the car, and ran to the back door. I knocked three quick rounds and heard Tiffany yell, "I'm coming!"

Seconds later the door opened, Tiffany looked up at me, rolled her eyes, and quickly headed back through the kitchen to the living room leaving me at the door. I could tell she was upset and that normally wasn't a good sign for me. She sat on the couch, picked up a magazine, and started reading. I yelled from the kitchen, "Tiffany, I made a song about Deshaan! I want to take him to the studio to hear it!"

Irritably and without looking up, she said, "No."

"Why?!"

"He's on punishment and he is not allowed to leave his room."

She was still seated in the living room and I was standing in the kitchen.

Again I pleaded. "Can Deshaan please go with me to the studio? I made a song about him. I'm not taking him somewhere to play. I understand he's grounded, but he's my son, too."

Tiffany hurriedly got off the couch and walked toward me. She stopped less than a foot in front and me and said, "I said no!'"

I continued to plead, stressing that I wasn't taking him to a park or a toy store. "I just want him to hear the song I made."

"No," she said. "And I won't tell you again."

I walked closer to her, my anger rising. This time I demanded, "Let me take my son to the studio."

"You get out of here right now or I'm calling the police," she said.

I was still begging when she picked up the phone to call the police. Joe grabbed my arm and said, "Let's get out of here."

He was right. I went too far with my hollering and ordering Tiffany around. I swiftly turned and walked into Deshaan's room which was connected to the dining room. He looked up at me and then quickly looked back down at a toy he had in his hand. Not only did he look sad, he also looked disappointed. I wasn't sure if he was disappointed that he couldn't go with me, which was something he loved to do, or if he was disappointed that I yelled at his mother.

"I'm sorry," I stated, then I turned in shame and left.

I was about to start the car when I looked at Joe. "I have to wait until the cops come," I said. "I don't want them to just show up at my job and arrest me, because there's no telling what she might say to them."

"I think we should just get out of here!" Joe screamed.

But I refused. Two cop cars were at the apartment within five minutes. I've always felt like they rushed to the scene, because it was a white woman who called them. The first officer jumped out of his car. I began to get out of mine so I could explain myself. The cop motioned with his hand for me to stop and said loudly, "Sir, get back in the car."

For a quick second I thought he was implying that I could leave, but then I noticed that one of the cop cars was blocking me in. I sat confidently for three or four minutes. One of the cops stepped back outside of the apartment, as if he had been told to watch me. Soon afterwards the other cop came out of Tiffany's apartment and headed toward my car.

"Step out of the car, sir," he demanded. I did as I was told.

"Turn around and put your hands on the roof," he ordered.

Once I had my hands on the car he started to pat me down.

"Do you have any weapons on you?"

"No," I replied.

I tried to explain the situation and most of all, I tried to find out why I was being arrested. The officer cut off every question I asked.

"Put your hands behind your back," he said, and then he began reading me my rights while putting handcuffs on me. As the cop led me toward the police car Joe asked if someone could tell him why I was being arrested.

"He hit the young woman in the house," a cop replied.

"Officer, I was right there. I saw it all, he did not hit her," Joe answered.

The cop stopped and said to me, "Don't you move." He asked the other cop to go back inside and figure out who was lying.

I began to wonder if I really did hit her. Questions and thoughts swirled around in my head. Maybe I was too angry to remember. Why didn't the cop ask me what happened? I don't have bail money and I don't have anyone to bail me out. How am I going to explain this to my boss? The cop returned from inside the apartment.

"Okay, she has changed her story," he said. "Tiffany is now saying that this man was yelling at her and while pointing at her, he connected his finger to her forehead."

Again I thought to myself: Maybe I did touch her and I don't remember, because I was so upset. In the end it obviously didn't matter whether or not I remembered what happened. A finger to the forehead was enough to charge me. The cop continued to escort me to his car.

"Watch your head," he said as he steered me into the back seat.

The patrol car had a nauseating smell that confirmed I was going to jail. There was something about the smell of a police car that made me feel weak, hopeless, scared, and trapped. The smell lingers in my memory even today, and for years it was accompanied by the haunting statistic that said my chance of returning to jail was well over 85 percent. That night, as I stood outside Tiffany's apartment with the police officer, I thought, how did something so right go so wrong so fast?

I sank deeply into a dark-blue funk. My life seemed adrift, out of control. This happened years before I would read a book called The Proverbial Cracker Jack: How to Get Out of the Box and Become the Prize by Dale Henry. Henry's book taught me that something new that affects your life happens every day and many of these things will not go the way you want. Henry said, "We should look at obstacles as opportunities."

I did not have this insight yet. I saw the incident with Tiffany as confirmation that I was helpless and had no control over my life. I could have the best intentions, I thought, and still end up in jail.

Lockport, New York was a small city with the Niagara County Jail located downtown and an undersized federal prison facility on the outskirts of the city. The federal prison was home to people serving less than a couple of years. They took me downtown to the small county jail. The officer pulled up to a garage door. He spoke something into his walkie-talkie and then a couple seconds later the door began to rise. He parked in a space near an entrance, then got out the car, walked over to my door, and opened it.

"Let's go," he demanded.

He escorted me inside to a small glass window where a man sat on the other side. The officer then took off my handcuffs and commanded that I step up to the glass.

"Empty your pockets please," the man said.

"The officer took everything out of my pockets earlier," I replied.

He ordered that I give him my shoe laces, my belt, my watch, my necklace, and my coat. The arresting officer requested that I put my hands up on the wall near the window. Again he patted me down, asking, "Any hidden weapons or drugs?"

I was frightened and I was sure they could hear the fear in my voice as I answered, "No."

He ushered me to a small jail cell about ten feet long and five feet wide. It had a small, steel, silver sink and a toilet with lots of stains around it. Because it had no toilet seat, it just looked like a dirty hole in the floor with soggy toilet tissue in it. The only other thing in the cell was a wooden cot suspended from the wall. It was cold and the cot had no sheets. The floor was made of cement, but it looked like rusted metal.

I had been arrested a couple of times in Lockport, because of my habit of fighting, but I still shuddered in anticipation of hearing the sound I hated more than any I had ever heard before: the chilling, clanging sound that marked the beginning of loneliness, the closing of the door that turned my cell into a cage.

Before leaving, the cop said he would try to get the judge to come down before she left that day, otherwise I would be shipped to the federal prison in the morning. Of course I prayed that the judge would come, knowing that it would be a nightmare to stay where I was all night. I wanted to cry, but I was a man, and my pride wouldn't allow me to show any emotion. I walked up to the bars and peered through them. The other cells were empty. It was really cold. I went over to the bench and sat down hesitantly because of how worn and corroded it looked. I leaned forward and began to pray. I didn't normally pray during the day–unless I was in trouble. As I prayed, I waited for some type of noise that signaled someone was coming up to my cell to say the magic words, "You're free!"

Finally, an older white woman with dark-black, short hair stood in front of my cell. She asked politely, "What happened here, young man?"

I explained the whole story in a humble and apologetic way.

"I believe you although I stand strongly against any type of domestic violence— physical or verbal," she said. "Do you have anyone to bail you out?"

"No, ma'am."

"How much money do you have on you?"

"About eight dollars."

"I will set your bail at fifty dollars. Do you have someone to bring you the rest?"

"Not sure, ma'am."

She gave me a court date which was two weeks away. She had a grin on her face as if she felt sorry for me, but still wanted to punish me just in case I had pushed Tiffany or had been verbally abusive. It took the guards another two hours to let me use the phone to call someone to bail me out. I wasn't sure who to call. During this time my mother didn't have a phone or money to bail me out. I hadn't spoken to my father in over two years. My grandparents couldn't afford to help me. So I called Joe and within a couple of hours he came to bail me out. Even after the officer told me that someone had posted bail it took another couple of hours just to let me go.

Two weeks later I was at the courthouse waiting for my case to be called. Every time I went to go to court it was like going to the DMV or filing for unemployment: there was always a long wait. Court started at 9 AM., but I didn't get called until about 1 PM. I couldn't afford a lawyer so I had to use a public defender. I knew from my previous experiences that public defenders didn't really help much. The ones I had met never seemed to like their jobs and weren't that interested in going to bat for someone like me who they would probably label a troublemaker. This public defender was no different from the others.

I had been in the courtroom for hours when the judge finally called my name. I walked over to a table where my public defender was standing. I was nervous. The judge had sent about 30 percent of the people who faced her that day to jail. Unlike a lot of judges I had gone before, she seemed to be very observant and caring, although I felt she had little tolerance for people who lied. I planned to tell the truth, so I hoped that was enough. She was the same judge who had spoken with me while I was in jail. I told my story again, she paused for a moment, grabbed a stack of papers and began to look them over. I assumed the stack was made up of copies of my arrest records. After looking them over, she looked down at me and said, "After reviewing your records, it looks as if you have an anger problem."

My heart began to beat really fast. I was terrified she was about to put me back in jail.

"You will serve twenty-six weeks of anger-management classes," she said.

I looked to my public defender to say something in response and he simply said, "Thank you, Your Honor."

That one decision changed my life again and helped to make me a better father. I would learn a lot about who I was as a result of those classes.

I showed up for my first anger-management class in a building near the downtown area. I stepped onto a very small elevator crowded with six other men. When the doors opened, we all walked out onto the fifth floor. We ended up in a tiny classroom where we were greeted by a man who looked to be about 50 years old. Some of the men had been taking the classes for weeks, while a couple of them were new like me.

"Hello, please be seated. I'm Ken," the instructor said. "Let's go around the room, and each of you state your name and tell us why you are here."

Some of the guys had beaten their wives. One had punched a hole in a wall. I didn't feel any of them was as innocent as I was.

When Ken finally got to me, he said, "So, Mr. Benson, why are you here?"

I was a little cocky, sustained by my belief that in some way I was better than the other guys. I told my story in less than a minute. Ken gave me a weird look and then continued to ask others around the room the same question. For twenty-five weeks I refused to admit any wrongdoing on my part. It wasn't until the last week that something shifted for me. At the beginning of the last class Ken pulled me aside.

"Mr. Benson, I can't give the judge a good recommendation on your behalf. Maybe the reason you are here isn't solely because of the argument between you and Tiffany. Maybe your main reason for being here is your stubbornness in denying your anger. At any rate, I'll give you one last chance to talk about this, but you have to be honest."

I gazed around the room. Everyone was staring back at me. At first I wanted to just make up something to get him off of my back, but something inside of me finally wanted to face the truth. I put my head down into my hands and thought to myself, Perhaps I am an angry person. If so, why? Either way, it's time for me to confront the issues. After that, something magical happened.

Ken began asking me about my childhood. "Were you angry as a kid? Did someone hurt you and if so, who?"

I continued to cover my face with my hands until he asked me about my mother. "Did your mother hurt you?" he asked.

I looked up and glared into his eyes. I felt the anger and hurt rise up in me. "Don't ever say anything about my mother!" I shouted.

He didn't hesitate, "Did she hurt you when you were young?"

All of a sudden, for the first time in 10 years I could feel the belt hitting me. I touched my arms as if the belt marks were there, swollen and reddish from the beating. I had suffocated those horrifying memories for longer than I realized. Up to this point I hadn't faced the issue. Was it right? Were the whippin's justified? I wondered. After all, I was a difficult child growing up in a household with a woman who did not know how to alter my behavior because she was dealing with her own rage and pain. I had taken on my mother's rage.

The conversation with Ken was a turning point, the first time I looked my past dead in the eye. It was a major breakthrough, but it was just the start of my recovery. Unfortunately it would not be the end of my rage. It would take years before I realized how very fortunate I was to stand in front of that particular judge and to end up in the class with that particular counselor. Normally judges had given me fines that I couldn't afford to pay. This judge had taken the time to listen and offer a solution that could make me a better person.

I'm often startled to see how young people are treated by judges and the court system. It makes me wonder how many teachers, judges, and parents actually take the time to understand why a child is misbehaving and how, as leaders, our behavior affects that child. We've been taught to use whippin's, incarceration, fines, and suspensions as acts of punishment for our young people, but the underlying solution should be trying to find out why the child misbehaving in the first place. Of course this takes more time and effort than the "quick" solutions we've become accustomed to such as whippin's and incarceration, which more often than not have a negative effect to the solution.

CHAPTER 8

FAMILY INFLUENCE IN THE 'HOOD

My mother and father had a couple of things in common: they both were young when they had me, and both of them had an attitude problem. My father fought on the streets a lot. He had a quick temper. He was also on his high school wrestling team and ran track. They just couldn't get along, so, as I mentioned earlier, when I was 2 years old he left to join the Marines. After he left the Marines, he moved down south to Baton Rouge, Louisiana where he began to build a new family. He got married and he and his new wife Mary have two daughters.

Mary and I didn't get along for many years. She called me a "cry baby all the time. For instance, if she was cooking and I told her that I didn't like something, she would say, "Stop acting like a cry baby and just eat."

This name calling began when I was 8 years old and continued until I was about 20. I'm guessing she did it because I reminded her of my mother. Needless to say, my mother didn't like Mary either. Mary was only mean to me when my father wasn't around, and when she was mean, I called my mother and told her the first chance I got. One summer while I was visiting my father I met a young woman who lived in his community. She and I were at the laundry mat one day when my father's wife approached me and began teasing me, calling me names.

"Jaz is whack," she said. "No one likes a loser!"

I was so embarrassed that I ran out of the laundry mat, but I could still hear her yelling, "Go tell your momma, cry baby! You act just like a baby. Go cry to your momma!"

I did exactly what she said I would do. I ran back to the apartment, cried, and called my mother. I was still talking to her when my stepmother walked in.

"Here, my mother wants to speak with you," I said in between sobs.

My mother told her that if I wasn't on a plane by the next day she would be on one and she was going to beat her ass. Of course I was shipped off the following day. As a child, I saw my father about once a year. On occasion he came back to The Falls to visit family, but when he visited, he rarely came to see me. I always knew when he was coming and I got excited about his visit. I talked about him all the time to my friends—how I had a father with money and how much he cared about me. Honestly, I didn't know if my father had money or not. In my mind I had someone who loved me and who wasn't in the 'hood. I believed that one day he'd come and rescue me. Even today, as an adult, I feel that way.

My father visited The Falls for a week at a time. Out of that week, he visited me for about two hours. Still, those two hours were precious to me. I didn't understand why my mother yelled at him so much when he came by. As I became older, however, it made sense. She hated that he didn't care about me and that I cared too much for him.

I had a chance to go visit him about three times as a kid. Once was the time when my stepmother embarrassed me in the laundry mat and my visit was cut short. The other two times were for about four days each. One of those periods, when I was 12 years old, my father hit me for the first time. I had always heard from my mother that he had an anger problem, but we weren't around each other enough for me to witness it. It happened when he took me school shopping while I was visiting him in Baton Rouge. I was acting like a spoiled brat, because he wouldn't buy me this outfit I wanted. I poked my lips out, crossed my arms, eyed the ground, and refused to talk to my dad while we were in the store. I wanted an expensive jumpsuit from JCPenney's, but he made me get a no-name jumpsuit from a hole-in-the wall store. Now when I look back, I think he couldn't afford what I wanted, but he couldn't bring himself to tell me that. We left the small store that reminded me of Goodwill and headed to his house. We didn't speak to each other for the first 10 to 15 minutes until I changed the radio station that he was apparently listening to. He had it on a station that played old-school R&B music, but I wanted to listen to hip hop. After I changed the station, he changed it back. Again, I changed it. He looked at me with his piercing eyes, then turned back to the oldies and said, "Touch it again and see what happens."

I paused for a moment and then boldly changed it again. For the remaining half hour drive back to his house we didn't talk to each other. By the time we pulled up to his place, I was ready to eat and watch the new B.E.T. channel. B.E.T. was the biggest thing since Atari. We had MTV, but this was before MTV started putting black music into their rotation. My cousin Anthony and I used to stay up to 7in the morning just to record two to three R&B or hip hop videos on MTV. You could sometimes catch Michael Jackson or Prince, but it normally stopped there. By the time we arrived at the house I had forgotten what had happened between me and my father regarding the radio station. I ran into the house and he walked in behind me. I ran up to the stove to see what his wife had cooked and as soon as I turned around I saw the palm of his hand coming forcefully toward my forehead. His hand was actually coming at me fast, but it seemed to be moving in slow motion. Bam! I fell back into the sink. I looked up in shock and by then he was in a stance like he was ready to fight.

"Come on, I'm about to teach you a lesson," he barked.

I paused for a moment. It felt like 10 minutes had passed. I could see everything in the kitchen in greater detail than ever before. Tiny spots on the floor stood out. Small cracks in the ceiling looked huge. Then I looked at him again. I charged at him and started swinging as if my life depended on it, but nothing was hurting him. He grabbed me and threw me into the dining room. I hit the floor and within that brief moment I discovered that my anger had limitations. I looked to the left and glanced at his dining room glass table. I knew I could grab the sheet of glass and end the fight. I was used to fights without limitations, but that day I learned that love would prevent me from physically hurting anyone close to me. I normally did anything to survive, but this time I decided to just take the whippin' like a man.

As I began to get up my father yelled, "You better stay down!"

I got up and he grabbed me. This time he hurled me into the hallway.

"Stay down," he yelled again.

I got up. He grabbed me again, and dragged me down his small hallway and tossed me into the guest bedroom.

"Stay down I said!"

Again I stood up and sprang toward him. He hit me a couple of times and all of a sudden I was falling back directly into an old, steel-gray heater connected to the wall. The bang to my head crippled me to the point I could not get up. I fell asleep against the warm heater.

The next day I was on a Greyhound bus back to The Falls. At least a year went by before I spoke to him again and about two years before I saw him. My mother was comfortable with us not talking considering she didn't like how much I cared for him. Still I looked up to my father my entire childhood. I think it was because he had the luxury of not living in the 'hood. He lived in a nice house in a peaceful neighborhood with neighbors he could trust. Later as an adult—in my early 20s—I began to look at him as a deadbeat dad. My resentment turned into frustration and then into anger. Yet I wondered, did he leave because I was a bad son? Was he ashamed of me, because of my scars and tattoos? And how could he live not knowing who I was, what I was doing, what made me smile, and what made me sad?

In my early 30s I began to understand and accept him for who he was and what he did. He had me at a young age. He didn't know much about being a father. As I prayed one day, I asked God, "Why me? Why did I have to grow up without a father?"

I didn't get an answer immediately, however, one day, while praying about my father again, I felt God touch me with a reply, "I am your Father. It had to happen this way. I don't need you to follow Man.

I need you to follow Me." Surprisingly I was not frightened by hearing a response. It was as if I had been waiting for it, half expecting it.

At that moment I understood that the Lord will sometimes take things away in an effort to teach us to listen to what He has planned for us. In my opinion we get so tied up focusing on what we don't have that we fail to appreciate what we do have, and we focus so hard on what Man wants us to do rather than what the Lord has planned for us. With the Lord's guidance we can accomplish anything—with or without money or a parent. It was a process, but in time, because of what I read and heard, I forgave my father, as well as others I felt hurt me in the past.

My father had a lot of family in The Falls. The Benson's are like a clan, there are hundreds of them in that area. One of the reasons I had to leave The Falls was because my last name is Benson. Anytime I went in front of a judge I wasn't just prosecuted on what I did, but also because of who I was. Don't get me wrong, the Benson's are one of the most loving families you will ever meet, but they don't take well to outsiders. They stick together. It didn't matter whether you sold drugs or worked at a chemical plant, when something went wrong, the Benson's supported you. They had a bad reputation when it came to selling drugs, but they're known for sticking together. Most of the Benson women had four to six children. The men averaged five to seven kids. The family bond was strong. If you fought one Benson, you had to fight ten. I was uncommon among the clan; I only had one child and I didn't sell drugs. I was always fearful of selling drugs, both because of what it did to my mother and also because judges were sentencing drug dealers to longer terms than convicted rapists.

As tough as I thought I was, I was horrified at the thought of spending serious time in jail. I saw first-time offenders get 10 years unless they took a plea bargain and told on a fellow drug dealer, but snitching came with high consequences. If you were released early after being arrested, people normally suspected you told on someone. In some cases, the cops actually told people that you talked, knowingly jeopardizing your life. Once you were released onto the streets and the cops put the word out that you snitched, the drug dealer you told on was coming for you.

I did fight like the Benson's, perhaps I fought even more than some of them. I could depend on them to watch my back and they could depend on me. Even the Benson women were tough and ready to crush any outsider that got in my way. For instance, if one of the Benson men got into a verbal or physical confrontation with a woman that wasn't related to the family, all he had to do was make a phone call and a Benson woman showed up, ready to fight the outside woman.

My cousin, "Biggie" stands out among the Benson's. We called him "Biggie," but he was just the opposite. He wasn't fat, but he was big. He had broad shoulders, over six feet tall, athletic, and weighed about 240 pounds. I watched him walk down the street in his boxers in the middle of winter with a bat in his hand, looking for a man who hit his sister. He was violent, but caring. Guaranteed, he could be counted on if something went down. The male Benson's ran to Biggie's sister Merice when we had problems with females. She was a true Benson, loyal to her family members. She once beat down two females after one of them put their hands on me.

We all had respect for my father's brothers and sisters. They didn't fight, but they lectured us a lot when we got into trouble. My Uncle Pop and Uncle Philip were my favorites. For some reason, when I turned 17, they began to look out for me. It started with Uncle Philip. At the time he lived with this old man named Major. Major helped raise Philip and when Major grew old, Philip took care of him. Since Uncle Philip worked long hours, me and my cousins Tom and Biggie watched the house and looked after Major when Philip was at work. It was great, because it was like having the house to ourselves since Major didn't come out of his room often. After three months of hanging out there I started gradually moving in. Tom and I loved to watch videos and our favorite movie was Grease. We would recite all the words, sing all the songs, and dance to all the numbers. It was amusing for most of the people who visited to watch two tough boys dance and sing along to Grease. In no time, Uncle Philip's place became the local hang-out, especially for young women. One afternoon I came in from work and heard a lot of commotion coming from the basement. Tom ran up to me and said, "Biggie is running a whore house in the basement!"

I ran downstairs and saw about six men lined up waiting. Biggie was at the front of the line collecting money. I walked past everyone and noticed a white woman with blond hair lying on a small bed, holding her legs wide open with no pants or panties on. I watched as guys just walked up to her, pulled down their pants, and inserted their penises in her vagina, then humped her until they had an orgasm.

"This isn't right!" I screamed to Biggie.

"Try it before you knock it," he said dryly.

"Hell no! Uncle Philip is going to kill us!" I screamed.

Biggie was unmoved. "Here is a beautiful woman with her legs spread open, and you're going to pass it by. Here's a condom," he said.

I paused for a moment, took the condom, and then walked up to the woman. I unzipped my pants, put on the condom, and began to awkwardly have sex with the stranger lying limp on the bed. I looked up at her; she seemed to be drunk or drugged. "Hey, Jaz," she said. I was puzzled when she called me by my name. I didn't recognize her. I closed my eyes and tried to get past the fact that this was wrong. I felt guilty and had some sympathy for the young woman. I felt like I was raping her. I remember thinking that we all might go to jail for this. After stroking her a few times, I stopped. I opened my eyes and looked into hers. Even though she had a slight smile on her face, she looked sad. I wanted to say sorry but didn't want anyone but her to hear it. Quickly, I backed away and ran upstairs.

Like I normally did, I fell asleep on the couch. The next day, a rumor quickly spread that the woman on the bed had crabs. That night I saw a teeny, tiny crab for the first time in my life. I didn't see it on me, but on the couch. It was creepy looking. Tom grabbed a shoe and hit it. It took a long time for it to die.

This type of atmosphere became a norm at Phil's place. He worked long hours and put me in charge. Most of the time, believe it or not, I was scared to disappoint him.

I was about 18 years old when I became close to another uncle named Pop. Pop didn't talk a lot, but somehow I knew what he was thinking. Pop was my father's youngest brother. Every now and then, Pop would let me drive his car. This was a big thing to me considering no one trusted me with their car besides my grandparents. Pop had four kids. His oldest son Lance lived with his grandmother. We didn't get along. I tried for a long time to get along with him, but each time Lance revealed himself as a thief and a liar. I felt sorry for Lance, unlike most of the Benson's who kept their distance from him. Even though Lance's mother was the babysitter who molested me when I was young, I never told him and never held it against him. I felt sorry for him, although I never understood why he and his father weren't closer. Pop was a great man. He was there for the family, not in a violent way, but in a caring and supportive way.

Phil and Pop had a lot to do with me changing my life. They were male role models in my life who inspired me to leave The Falls and be a better man. There were only two other people who protected me and inspired me to be a better man and those other people were my grandparents. My grandparents consistently came to my rescue when I was in trouble. They taught me to drive, and then pushed me to get a driver's license, a job, my own place, and eventually leave the 'hood.

Unfortunately, many kids in the 'hood don't have positive influences and role models who were working to make their dreams come true. Doctors and lawyers didn't live in my 'hood, and it was rare to see someone reading a book or getting a Master's degree. Due to the lack of examples of people striving to become better or achieve a fruitful, productive lifestyle legally in the 'hood, young people didn't have a lot of hope. Kids adapt to their surroundings. If hopelessness is the norm, children become hopeless, and then they have no reason to behave well in school, because without hope, they come to believe that nothing they do will impact their future.

CHAPTER 9

RELIGIOUS INFLUENCE IN THE 'HOOD

When I was about 22 years old I was sentenced to 30 days in jail in Ontario, Canada. I got arrested because immigration thought I was someone else. My cousin used to sell drugs in Canada. Whenever he crossed the border, without my permission, he used my name as well as my identification. A close friend of mine named Chill came to my house one day after taking my cousin Tom to Canada.

Chill said, "Jaz, I took Tom to Canada earlier today. Immigration refused us entry, because Tom didn't have appropriate identification. When they asked to see his I.D., he pulled out a couple of identification cards with your name on them."

I looked in my top dresser drawer where I kept old identification, like expired medical cards and noticed they were missing. For a brief moment I was upset, however, I got over it. Tom, like me, grew up in an unstable environment. For the most part we both did what it took to survive. But, understanding Tom's motives didn't help the awful relationship between me and Canadian Immigration. Although this wasn't the sole reason I was arrested, it was the spark that ignited a series of events resulting in my arrest.

While doing the 30 days, I figured I would be productive–exercise and read the Bible. I never really went to church consistently. Periodically I went with a friend or family member to their church which afforded me the opportunity to be introduced to different religions. My mother took us to church on special occasions and holidays until I was about 10 years old. My 30-day stint in jail was the first time I attempted to read the Bible without the assistance of a pastor or preacher. I would lie on the top bunk bed and read Scripture for hours at a time. I highlighted things that I didn't understand. The goal was to talk with a pastor and ask for clarification once I was released.

I wanted clarification on things like, was Jesus really the son of God or are we all the sons of God? Was Jesus just a man? How do we know for sure He was resurrected? How is it that we rely on so many theories, visions, and opinions of people in the Bible given some of them go back thousands of years? From the story of Adam and Eve to Noah's Ark, how can we trust one man's theories or visions? How do we know there's a Heaven or Hell if no one came back to tell us about it? The Lord seems to be unpredictable so how is it that we can define when He's coming and how the earth will end? There are so many religions, how do we know which is the right one?

After being released I decided to go to church, but the question was which church? Among my friends, there were all kinds of churches and religions represented. My friends and I created a unique clique. Most of us had little in common, but we got along great. Our uniqueness complemented each other. We called ourselves the 122 Click. Anthony, my cousin and best friend since I was 5 years old, dressed in hip-hop clothes, loved to sing, was smooth with the women, and still loves to club hop. Brian was raised in the church, dressed in suits all the time, wouldn't drink or smoke, and was the comic of the crew. Tom was the thug and risk taker. Ace dressed in preppie clothes and was all about the women. Otis had a neo-soul type style— sometimes long, curly hair, sometimes short—and is a tattoo artist who has over 50 tattoos and piercings. He was the philosopher of the crew. Most of us were slim, about six feet, and mainly on the lighter side, but Chill was a little on the heavy side, dark-skinned, and wore long braids. He had a big heart and was the first one to have a nice car. He also was the one who kept us all in line. Black was short and dark-skinned, loyal, loved to make music, and had his own style in clothes, which was kind of a mixture of preppy and hip hop. Taiwan was the B-Boy with a low tolerance. He had a career and was family driven. Oscar was the oldest, knew how to fix everything, had two nice cars, and only dated white women. All of them went to different churches and for the most part, each had a different religion.

Each week I went to a different church with one of my friends. I started with Brian. At his church I carefully watched the members run around, crying, speaking in tongues, and praising God. Tom came with us. The pastor requested that people who wanted to become new members approach him at the altar. We got up and headed toward the front of the church. Moments later, everyone but me was jumping up and down, crying and screaming while worshipping. Tom and I stood next to one another just staring at everyone around us. A man walked up to us. He touched Tom's lower back and immediately Tom started jumping and screaming. I was wondering if he was faking it. Soon the man approached me and calmly placed his hand on my lower back, asking me to allow the Holy Ghost to flow through me. I didn't feel anything. Did that mean I was a bad person? Did it mean I just didn't know how to relax and allow the Holy Spirit to flow through me? Or was everyone just faking it and didn't know it? Either way I continued to just stand in one place, watching the people around me. Soon the man walked on to another person.

Tom was still jumping up and down, but I tried to get his attention by staring at him with a sarcastic grin on my face. I finally caught his attention and he looked over at me, winked his eye, and continued to scream and jump up and down. As we walked out the church, the Pastor greeted everyone by shaking their hands and nodding. When I approached him, I asked him one of the unanswered questions I had been carrying around since jail, is there really a place called Hell? I was confused because it seemed to me that in the Old Testament, Hell was considered the result of a negative or violent act by a human being versus an actual place as described in the New Testament.

"Hell is a place where sinners go when they die," the Pastor said.

"How do you know?" I asked, not meaning to be disrespectful at all, but I was anxious to get an answer to the question that had been bothering me for some time.

"It's written in the Bible," the pastor replied.

His answers didn't sit well with me, so I decided to continue my journey in search of the right church. The following week I went to Anthony's church and I repeated my question to his Pastor.

"Hell is not an actual place, but the result of a negative or violent act by a human being," the Pastor said. I told him the answer I received from the other Pastor.

"I know the Bible and there are false prophets out there," he said.

I was surprised because basically he was telling me that the other Pastor was wrong. I went to three other churches. Some Pastors said Hell wasn't a real place and some said it was; this was disturbing to me.

How is it that they could all read the same book but come up with different answers and point fingers at each other when they were supposed to be on the same team? My experience with these Pastors pushed me to change my tactic. One quiet evening I got on my knees and began to pray. So many puzzling questions ran through my head. How would someone know what Hell is if they've never been there? Don't get me wrong, I understand that there have been plenty of prophets who had premonitions about many things, including Hell, but that still wasn't enough for me. Why did most of the Pastors give me different answers? During this time I learned about meditation.

I was trying to mediate one night, following from memory the process I had read on how to meditate. Without realizing it at first I slipped into a trance. There was a stillness I had never experienced before. I let go of all the noise in the world and heard sounds I had never heard before. It was like being in a beautiful field— no houses, no flowers—only wind blowing weeds that sparkled from the sun, and I heard this wind hit the weeds and I heard it as it moved through the air. This was when the Lord delivered a message to me that went something like this:

"You've cried many nights about being alone, not having a father for guidance, or a mother to lay your head on her shoulder. I'm your Father, let me guide you; rest your head on My shoulder. You have a lot of questions about what was and what will be. Unnecessary questions will be left unanswered. You have a purpose and this purpose will lead you down a road that will not judge people. Your journey will bring religions, politicians, and races together. You will inspire my children no matter what their background is. Follow me and you'll have no more questions."

After that experience, I began to meditate at least once a month. The goal was to open myself up to listening versus complaining to the Lord and asking for help. I began to see how influential religion was in black communities. I have watched the number of mega churches grow, but I know that many followers need something more quaint and personal than a humongous place of worship. Most religions teach people to love and worship a Higher Power, which is great, but my meditation, praying, and pondering has led me to getting as close to the Lord as I can when I'm alone and quiet, away from the noise created by the world. I believe that the Lord has a purpose for everyone, and we can read the Bible until we're blue in the face, but if we're not listening to what He wants from us it's just worshipping and nothing else.

Later, when I opened my bookstore with a large religion section, my Sundays became very interesting. On many occasions I'd have a Buddhist or a Muslim in the store and sooner or later they'd get into a debate around myths about the Bible. Every time this scene played out, I'd think that we were all created by a Higher Power. It doesn't matter if you call Him Buddha or God, we are all His children. I look at this Higher Power simply as a perfect Father who wants us not to judge, but to understand, learn, and respect each other.

When I was growing up in The Falls, everyone knew the Pastors of the community. A lot of Pastors are like celebrities now, constantly building larger and larger churches and becoming bigger than celebrities themselves. Churches used to be more intimate, where a member facing a problem he or she couldn't solve could just call the Pastor for inspiration. Today, we seem to have lost the advantage of calling the Pastor, so we end up calling somebody who has the same issues we have. I have made it my goal with my business to create a movement that operates similar to the way religion affects the urban community. I want to create a movement that inspires people to better themselves in regards to health, spiritual growth, relationships, financial responsibility, and in other matters that impact the total well-being of a person. The majority of people going to church in the urban community are still leaving church and returning to their homes to face the same financial, health, and family problems. I am not trying to bad-mouth the Church, I'm just simply saying that the Church can't do it alone. It's time for a transformation in terms of the way help is delivered to the 'hood. It's time for a new movement.

CHAPTER 10

LOVE IN THE 'HOOD

Around the age of twenty I started dating a woman who dramatically changed my life. I can appreciate her today even more than ever, but at the time, I put her through hell. Korena lived in Canada, but she was from Nigeria. I didn't know what to expect from her when we first met. She was beautiful, highly intelligent, and fun to be around. Before we dated, she went out with my close friend, Otis's younger brother, a guy named Nate. I wasn't that close to Nate; we saw each other once or twice a year. Korena traveled most of the time with her friend April. Otis, my best friend and the philosopher of the group, dated April. Since I had my own place they all occasionally came by to hang out, but Nate never came with them.

Korena liked stopping by my place, and she complained a lot about Nate standing her up. It wasn't long before she quit him. Another friend of mine, Tom, pursued her and I don't know what happened, but it didn't work out. One night, after leaving a club in St. Catharine's, Ontario, we all hung out for a little while in Korena's car in the parking lot. When the girls were about to leave, I asked Korena if she would give me a hug. She got out the car and leisurely walked toward me. She had brown eyes that seemed to glow. As we hugged, her scent lingered. I can still recall her scent. It wasn't her perfume or soap; it was her natural scent that I was attracted to. I held her for about 30 seconds and then gradually, I released my grip from around her waist. She looked up at me with her beautiful brown eyes and I bent forward and kissed her. We kissed passionately for about a minute. When we stopped, she walked backwards to her car. She had a slight smile that said without words, "It was a great kiss." She got in her car and took off. Before this, I wasn't really interested in Korena.

While driving home, I wondered if that kiss was driven more by my hormones than by my heart. Korena continued to come by my place and eventually we began dating. One night Otis, April, Korena, and I had a conversation on the phone that intrigued me. We talked about oral sex.

"I'm comfortable going down on a man," Korena said.

On one hand I wanted her even more because of that comment. What man wouldn't? On the other hand, I lost some respect for her, because she was so comfortable talking to me and my friend about oral sex so early in our relationship. I didn't realize it at the time, but that conversation was nothing more than her telling a young, horny boy something she thought he wanted to hear. Unfortunately, Korena's experience with men had generally been bad. She was used to men leaving her. Even though she was 18 years old, she was naïve about men from the 'hood like me.

Was I attracted to Korena for all the wrong reasons? It wasn't just the sex or what she said on the phone. She was also fun to be around, but the cornerstone of our relationship was the fact that she provided something my life lacked: comfort. She had a beautiful house in Canada. When I visited her, I never wanted to leave. I wasn't used to resting my head in a place where you could barely find a stain on the wall. Her basement was the size of my apartment and it was beautifully furnished. She drove a new Ford Taurus. At most there were two people in my entire extended family that had new cars. Most of us drove vehicles that could barely make it up the street without overheating. She drove me and my friends anywhere we asked without complaining.

As time passed, Korena lovingly changed me for the better by gently offering advice and by using her own life to inspire me. For instance, she took education seriously. I had been kicked out of school in the 10th grade for multiple reasons, including fighting, bad grades, being late, and just not showing up for class. The year before I began dating Korena, my grandparents convinced me to go back and get my G.E.D. Next, Korena persuaded me to go to college and get a degree. I hadn't been to school for at least three to five years before agreeing to go to college.

But I was distracted. It bothered me that she had dated Nate. Even though Nate and I weren't close friends, we were friends. Our clique was strict about dating each other's ex-girlfriends and Nate was my best friend's brother. From time to time we all sat around and did what most men do: we talked about women. Before Korena and I started dating, her name would come up and Nate would say things like, "Korena and I have great sex, but she calls me too much!" So I had already painted a picture of who Korena was prior to us dating.

It also bothered me that she lived across the border. The Canadian border and young black men didn't go well together. The border patrol seemed to think all young black men were drug dealers. Whenever Anthony crossed the border, he gave them the upmost respect, but with me, it depended on my mood. In all honesty though, some of my troubles at the border were not caused by the patrols. For one, my cousin who had a record for selling drugs used my name a lot while crossing the border. He had a few warrants, so he used my name if they pulled him over. The border then had a difficult time separating our records. Once they showed me a folder with my cousin's face on it and my name. After that they started demanding that every time I crossed; I had certain updated documents like a certified birth certificate, police records, or a driver's license. When I didn't have all these things, or if they weren't updated, they made me wait for hours while threatening to put me in jail. So basically every time I crossed the border and got pulled over, they would make me wait for hours while threatening to put me in jail so they could send me back to the States.

I would sometimes give them a reason to hound me, again, depending on my mood. One evening Anthony and I had a show in Canada. Every now and then clubs in Canada paid us to perform. The opportunity to make the gig depended on whether or not we were able to cross the border. We had to drive over the Rainbow Bridge which separated the United States and Canada. I always felt uptight while crossing the bridge. That night while on the bridge caught in traffic, I stared at the roaring waters of The Falls. I began to worry, wondering if this time they were going to let me cross. Anthony always taunted me, telling me to be nice to the immigration officers. He demanded that when the officers asked a question, we look them in the face and reply immediately.

He would say, "When they ask us a question, respond like we were singing in harmony…say it together!"

On this particular trip, we pulled up to a little booth on the Canadian side. A young man with a stoic face said, "Citizenship?"

"American," we replied in harmony.

"Where are you going?" the man asked.

"We have a show at a club called Palm Groove," we replied.

"ID please," the man said.

We both handed the man our driver's licenses.

"Do either of you have a criminal record?"

"No, sir," we both replied.

He began to type something into a computer he had in front of him. Soon after, he handed Anthony a pink piece of paper and our licenses and demanded that we pull over to the left near a row of offices.

As we pulled over, two officers approached us. They had come from an office building near the bridge, "Give us your keys and enter the glass doors," one man ordered.

We walked into the office and a husky white man with red hair started asking us a series of questions. By then I was frustrated. I needed the money that the club was going to give us to pay bills. Anthony appropriately answered each question. After about the fourth question, I asked, "Are you going to let us over or not?"

"No, but sit back and relax, because you're going to be here for a while," the officer responded.

"Hell no," I said, heading toward the door.

"You can't leave until I say so!" The officer yelled.

I ignored him and walked out the door. I looked back and noticed the officer jumping over the counter. I ran back toward the bridge. After I got almost halfway across the Rainbow Bridge I stopped and turned around. The officer was running after me.

"I'm legally back in the United States now. If you touch me, I might throw you off this bridge!" I hollered.

He stopped about 10 feet in front of me, turned around, and walked back to his office. A couple of minutes later I walked into the US Immigration Office. By then the Canadian side had called and told them that I ran out of their office.

"Citizenship?" the woman asked.

"American," I replied.

"Why did you run out of the office?" she asked.

"Because I'm tired of them harassing me for no reason. I didn't do anything."

"Go ahead," she said.

I was ignorant about what the border patrols could do and how this would affect my relationship with Korena. In a way, I didn't care.

One day I went to a women's department store with my sister Thika. I wanted to buy her a couple of outfits for school. She quickly picked out two shirts and a pair of pants. We approached the sales clerk and handed her the clothes.

"Hey, Melissa!" Thika yelled with excitement.

"Hi, Thika." the girl replied.

"This is my brother Jaz. Jaz, this is Melissa." Thika said.

Melissa was beautiful.

"Nice to meet you Jaz," she said with a smile. "Follow me, I'll ring y'all up. I'll give you my employee discount," she said and walked away.

During this time Thika was living downstairs from me with our grandparents. I had a small apartment upstairs. I drilled a small hole in the floor one day and ran my grandparents cable and telephone line through it. On occasion Melissa would call Thika. One day, while Thika was out, Melissa called and we talked briefly. From there we became friends.

This happened right before Korena and I started dating. Like with Korena, at the beginning I wasn't really into Melissa, but more into what she could do for me. I wasn't asking these women for money and things like that; they both offered me light in the midst of so much darkness in my life. For instance, when I visited Korena in Canada, it was like a vacation. I got to leave the ghetto for a while and stay at her nice home. Considering how far we lived from each other and the issues with the border, Korena and

I only saw each other about once a week, sometimes once every two weeks. Melissa, on the other hand, came to visit about three to four times a week. She also had a nice car and took me everywhere I needed to go. We were going to the same college which worked out perfect since Niagara County Community College was about 15 miles away from where I lived. Korena and Melissa's lives seemed to be peaceful, and they had loving families that supported them.

After about six months, my relationship with Korena became serious. To her, I was her boyfriend. I still didn't know what I wanted, but decided to commit to the relationship just because I was scared of not having her at all. At the same time that Korena and I got serious, Melissa demanded that I commit to our relationship as well.

I thought I'd make a decision between the two of them to avoid a lot of heartache and problems, but I could never decide, so I spent four years contemplating what to do. I was young and naïve about what it took to be a man and sustain a meaningful relationship, therefore, I did what some men do: I gambled and kept both of them. The first couple of years, I didn't know which one to choose. I wasn't man enough or mature enough to make a decision, so I went back and forth between two women for four years, but I fell in love with Korena. Even though we were fighting a lot, I fell in love with her heart. Many will ask why I didn't I just break it off with Melissa.

Melissa was there for me the majority of the time. We were both going to the same college. I rode to school with her most of the time and normally caught a bus home. I was scared to break it off with Melissa. I was selfishly scared of surviving without her. She didn't fight with me, and she was very easy going. She lived close by. She had a big house with a huge pool in the backyard. Being with her was like taking a vacation as well, but I wasn't in love with her, and I was sure she wouldn't stay around if I didn't call myself her boyfriend. Whenever I had a fight with Korena, Melissa would oddly show up and make me smile, but it felt more like a best friend relationship. It wasn't hard to balance the two relationships, because, after all, Korena lived in another country approximately an hour away. She and I only saw each other two to four times a month.

One Christmas Eve, Korena came down to pick me up and take me back to her place. I was really nervous that night. My instincts were running wild. Actually, it was like the Lord yelling at me all day telling me not to cross the border. It had been about six months since I last crossed, but before the night was over, it would be another turning point in my life that would teach me to believe in the three signs I'd been given that night not to cross the border.

I packed my clothes and Korena's presents in my bright red tote bag. I told Melissa that I had a show in Canada, and I would have to spend the night over there. About 8 PM I heard a knock at the door. I ran like a kid meeting Santa Claus for the first time. It was Korena. She greeted me with a big hug.

"Are you ready?" she asked.

"I'm ready, but a little scared to cross the border," I replied.

The phone rang. It was my Uncle Pop. He got called in to work and asked if I could pick up his girlfriend Maria from the airport. Pop was a great and well-respected man, but when it came down to relationships in our family, no one respected the rules of traditional marriage. Pop lived with his wife Catty. She didn't get along with a lot of people, but she and I were cool. I was loyal to Pop. "Korena, can you please take me to get Maria from the airport?" I asked.

"Yes, but, Jaz, we have to hurry, because we don't want to cross the border too late," she said.

Afterward I realized this was the first sign I'd been given. After about 10 PM there's not a lot of traffic driving into Canada which means the immigration officers have plenty of time on their hands to harass people.

The airport was in Buffalo, a half an hour away. We got to the airport around 9:30 PM and Maria was due to land at 9:40PM. After waiting for about 20 minutes we reviewed the airline schedule and found out that her flight was delayed. She wouldn't land until 11:45 PM. This was the second sign.

Finally Maria arrived and we took her to the hotel. Meanwhile I realized that I couldn't find my police clearance, so we went back to my place to look for it. Losing my police clearance was the final sign that I should not have attempted to cross the border. The border patrol had threatened to arrest me if I didn't have my police clearance the next time I tried to cross. A police clearance proved that I didn't have a criminal record and no drug-related activities, and considering that Tom, my cousin and best friend had used my ID a lot had drug charges, I needed the clearance. Korena and I looked and looked, but couldn't find the police clearance. I wanted to spend the weekend with her at her place so bad, not only because she had a beautiful home, but because it was a loving home. I wanted to eat at a table with all kinds of Christmas goodies. I wanted to get up in the morning and see presents under the Christmas tree. I wanted to witness a Christmas like I had only seen on TV.

"I'll hide in the trunk because they're not going to let me over," I said.

"Jaz, are you crazy?" she said.

"Think about it. You're from Canada. They're not going to pull you over if they think you're by yourself," I said. "How often do they check your trunk?"

"The Canadian side almost never checks my trunk," said Korena. "You don't have to get in the trunk. Besides, it's against the law, Jaz."

"It's against the law if we get caught," I said.

For the next hour I worked on convincing her to let me ride in the trunk. Finally she agreed. About 20 minutes later we pulled over a couple of blocks away from the Rainbow Bridge. I gave her a kiss and told her to pop the trunk. Again she argued that this wasn't a good idea. She even offered to stay at my place for the holidays, but she lived with her older and younger sisters and I knew she didn't really want to spend Christmas away from them. I gave her a kiss again and said, "It'll be all right. In 15 minutes it'll be over."

I stepped out the car and got into her trunk, which was pretty roomy. Korena gave me a sad look as I rested my head on my tote bag, then she shut the trunk. About five minutes later I yelled from the trunk, "How close are we?!"

"We're almost there. There are about two cars in front of us," said Korena.

Every time the car stopped, my heart raced. Moments later, I heard a man say, "Citizenship, ma'am?"

Korena answered nervously, "Canadian."

Following a series of questions, the officer said words that made my skin crawl, "Can you pull over, ma'am, to the building on the left?" Korena pulled up slowly.

"Korena, just go straight, far enough so I can jump out!" I yelled from the trunk.

"Where? Where?" she screamed.

"There's a hotel up on the right!" I hollered. "Pull over near it and pop your trunk and then go back to the bridge and act clueless, as if you misunderstood the directions." I heard a loud siren. "Hurry!" I yelled again.

An instant later the car stopped and the trunk popped open. I leapt out, looked behind me, and saw a bunch of flashing lights.

"Just go back to the bridge and act like you didn't understand," I said. "Don't mention me." I dashed through some bushes behind the old hotel. I ran as fast as I could down a dark street in Niagara Falls, Canada. I was familiar with those streets since I had dated a girl who lived near the border. After running for about fifteen minutes I slowed down to a walking pace. It was really dark, gloomy, and cold. There weren't a lot of street lights in the upscale residential neighborhood I was walking through. My goal was to stay away from main streets.

I was scared, afraid of what might happen to Korena. If they didn't see me get out the trunk she would be fine, I thought. After wandering for about 45 minutes I started searching for a pay phone. It was around 1996, before cell phones were popular or affordable in the 'hood. Now my instinct, or the Lord, was telling me to make my way to the other border (the Lower Bridge), which was only about twenty minutes away. It sounds crazy, but the way the bridge is set up I could get really close to the bridge without anyone seeing me and then run back across to the American side. But no, my mind was still set on making it up to Korena's home in St. Catherine's.

I saw a pay phone near a small gas station. I cautiously walked up to the phone, constantly looking both ways for any signs of police cars. I dialed Korena's home number and a recording said, "45 cents please." I dipped my cold hands into my pocket and found two quarters.

After four rings a voice said, "Waboso residence." It was Korena's older sister.

Nervously I asked, "Have you heard from Korena?"

"No, I thought she was with you," she replied.

"We got in a little trouble at the border. Can I come there and wait for her?" I asked.

Her sister hesitated and then answered, "Yes, but is Korena all right?"

"She's fine," I said, shivering and probably sounding worried.

I hung up the phone and went through the phonebook attached to the pay phone until I found a taxi service. I sat on a log outside of the gas station waiting. My hands were stiff and numb from the cold. I stuck my hands in my coat pockets, hunched over, and waited for the taxi. It took about 10 minutes to come.

"How much will it cost to take me to St. Catherine's?" I asked the driver before getting into the cab.

He looked me up and down and said, "Thirty dollars and you have to pay before we leave."

I only had twenty dollars on me. "Can you take twenty dollars, and I will give you ten more when I get there?"

He eyeballed me for a second and then said, "Come on!"

I was taking another gamble because I wasn't sure if Korena's sister would give me ten dollars, but the taxi was warm and I was thankful to be inside. I listened as the taxi driver told a dispatcher where he was going. We rode in silence for about 10 minutes. Then the driver said, "Are you all right? You're kind of quiet."

I eyed him in his rearview mirror. "Yes, I'm fine," I said.

Half an hour later I arrived at Korena's home.

"Hold on," I told the taxi driver. I stepped out the car and headed toward the front door of the house. Before I reached the doorbell, Korena's sister Esabelle opened the door.

"I can't believe what you did," she said.

I ignored her complaint. "Can I please borrow ten dollars for the taxi?"

"Hold on," she said, walking away. She returned a few seconds later with a ten-dollar bill in her hand. She walked pass me and went straight to the cab to give the money to the driver.

I stood at the door and watched her walk up to the taxi in the cold with no coat on as if she didn't trust me to give it to him. As soon as she got within 10 feet of me I pleaded, "Have you heard from Korena?"

"Yep, they have her at the border. She called a few minutes ago. She said border officials have been questioning her for the past two hours." She then began to ridicule me about what we did. I listened for the most part. She was very upset, but didn't scream. Eventually I heard someone coming through the front door. I jumped up and peaked out the window. I was praying that it was Korena…alone!

It was Korena, and she walked around the corner and went straight to her bedroom. I followed her. "Are you all right?" I asked.

"I'm all right. What about you?" she responded. I walked up to her and gave her a huge hug. I couldn't do anything but repeatedly apologize.

"I'm so sorry for what I put you through," I pleaded. She went on to tell me about how they kept trying to get the truth, but she stuck with playing clueless. She told them that she had never been told to pull over and she had a lot of things on her mind so she mistakenly went straight. She looked really shook up. My instinct, or The Lord, started screaming in my head that I should go home and again I refused. I fell asleep holding Korena in my arms.

I heard a knock at the door. It was about six in the morning. I knew it was immigration officers. I leaped out the bed and headed for a closet in the basement. Fearfully I tucked myself away behind a large chest.

I heard Korena's sister scream. That was a sign that they had a search warrant. I could hear people running above me. It had to be at least ten people upstairs running through the house looking for me. Moments later I heard them coming down to the basement.

"Search all the rooms down here!" I heard a man scream. Seconds later the door opened to the closet in which I was hiding. I saw the reflection of a flashlight.

"It's clear," a man yelled. Someone else asked, "Where is he?"

"I told you that my pulling up had nothing to do with Jaz," Korena responded.

"We checked with a taxi service and shortly after you were told to pull over, a man took a cab to your place," the cop stated.

I could still hear cops running around the apartment. I thought to myself, The Lord gave me warning signs and I ignored them. I had another opportunity to get away by crossing the lower bridge and I ignored it. The Lord was gracious enough to give me an additional chance in which I could have just left after I realized that Korena was alright, but again, I ignored Him!

"He is here somewhere. Keep looking," I heard a voice demand. I could hear Korena and her sister constantly telling the police to get out. Soon after, the closet door opened again. This time the cop came all the way in.

"Here he is," the cop yelled. About three more cops ran into the room and dragged me out. "You are under arrest," a cop told me. Sitting in the back of a police car, all I could think about was being away from Korena and my son. I heard a lot rumors about being arrested as an immigrant in Canada. The one that stood out the most was, "If an immigrant is arrested in Canada, he has to wait until the Queen comes to release him, and it could take years!"

Luckily the rumor wasn't true, although they were strict about immigrants committing a crime in their country. Around four o'clock that day, the Magistrate sentenced **me to 30 days in jail**. This would be the first and last time I had to go to jail for more than four days.

Korena tried to make my stay as comfortable as possible. She came and visited me at least twice a week. I called her collect about twice a day. She convinced me to use the time wisely by working out and reading the Bible.

Melissa came up to see me about three times. I was in school trying to get my Associate's Degree in Communications and I had a job working for a local pizzeria. Melissa went by both my school and my job and made up an excuse that I broke my leg while visiting my father in Baton Rouge, Louisiana. Thankfully, when I got out, I was able to finish school, and I still had my job.

Korena had a beautiful hotel room waiting for me when I was released. It was within walking distance after I crossed the bridge. She had Christmas gifts and holiday food waiting for me as well. I had planned on telling her the truth about my relationship with Melissa, but first I had to break it off with Melissa. Melissa came by my place the next day. She ran up to me and hugged me for about five minutes. I didn't want to hurt her. I wasn't sure how and when to tell her about Korena. Melissa was a little more sensitive than Korena. What I was doing might really hurt her in a way that could impact her life. I realized the nature of what I'd done was selfish and the long-term effect it could have on her regarding trust, love, men…more specifically, black men! On the other hand, Korena was strong. She was courageous enough to never talk to me again if she found out.

It took me a couple of months to finally tell Melissa. She was tougher than I thought. I think she had another boyfriend about two weeks later. She did, however, get really emotional when I told her. She held her face, cried, and then began to swing at me in a non-threatening way with her hands.

I didn't tell Korena about Melissa until we got into a fight one night. I became a pro at telling the truth about something I did wrong in the midst of a fight. Regrettably, this type of behavior would become a destructive pattern that I would resort to for years within other relationships. Korena's and my relationship, however, was never the same. My actions at the border and the infidelity would destroy our relationship. It wasn't until we broke up that I understood what it felt like to be in love with a woman.

Two weeks after we broke up, my friend and roommate Chris walked up to me and said, "Jaz, are you alright?"

"Of course I am. Why you ask?" I questioned him.

"Jaz, for the past two weeks, you been going straight to your room after you get home from school or work and then you don't come out." I hadn't noticed I'd been doing that until he mentioned it. It took me about four years to get over her.

When I used to get whippin's I was told not to cry while being hit. I was taught to match pain with aggression. A lot of men fall victim to this subliminal teaching. Instead of crying, we have a tendency to shut down, become either verbally or physically violent, or sometimes both. Some women are attracted to this behavior because they may have witnessed their fathers acting the same way which makes it acceptable or normal to them.

I'm a strong believer that in most cases, relationships can strengthen and survive. There's a healthy way and an unhealthy way to repair a broken relationship; the unhealthy way involves a woman who responds to a man by talking at him in an aggressive manner after she feels he has done something wrong. It's also unhealthy to hope the problem will just go away. On the other hand, the healthy way is to seek help through a relationship counselor. Not an entertainer like the ones we watch on TV who don't have any education, experience, or relationship-counseling training. Again, mind you, how we treat a person is a learned behavior. In most cases, people are taught to match aggression with aggression.

Like most animals, when threatened, we go into attack mode, ready to either fight back or just flee from the scene in an effort not to have to put up with it again. Nevertheless, sometimes, depending on the nature of the relationship, we have to deal with each other even when we feel vulnerable, but a little knowledge and education can help inspire a relationship. The great thing about being a human animal is that when challenged the right way, we have the capacity to change. After extensive relationship training, I began to host relationship forums, dialogs, and speaking engagements. The common issues that I heard pertaining to men were:

- Men are dogs
- Men cheat
- Men lie
- Men watch sports too much
- Men play video games too much
- Men don't know how to handle/manage money
- Men can be verbally and physically abusive

Many of these traits for men can largely be attributed to a lack of education on how to do things differently. I'm not making excuses for men, but simply stressing that the habits mentioned above have the ability to be altered with proper training and counseling. At the same time, a man has to want to adjust and a woman has to be patient and supportive enough to walk him through it.

One thing I found during my speaking engagements is that most women had an issue with the last sentence, "a woman has to be patient and supportive enough to walk him through it." What women don't realize is that they are the foundation for many successful relationships, but we're living in a time where women are fed up and tired of putting up with the negative actions of men. The conflict between men and women is a key thorn that haunts relationships in the African-American community! When the queen and king are separated, the castle is crippled.

The modern-day woman has to work just as hard as the man, which can cause a conflict compared to the roles of many successful previous traditional relationships. The common issues I heard pertaining to women were:

- Women nag too much
- Women are not supportive
- Women won't cook any more

- Women dress too provocatively
- Women use sex as leverage to control the relationship

In terms of these complaints, the first question to ask is, "Does my spouse have the potential to positively adjust his/her behavioral pattern?" Notice I avoided using the word "change." So many people are sensitive to the word "change" when it relates to a spouse or parent. Change is going to happen whether we're with someone or not. There is more of an advantage to do it while with someone, therefore, if the answer is "yes," the next question is, "Can I tolerate and be patient with him/her while he/she is rehabbing?" If the answer to the second question is "yes," then the last question to ask is, "Can I forgive him/her?"

Remember, we cannot fix anything by talking at each other. That's not to say there won't be arguments. For example, I remember my social studies teacher in high school. He was a dark-haired, old white man that seemed to wear the same old, grimy, gray slacks with a stained, white collared shirt. He rarely smiled. I recall being late to his class one day. As I walked into his classroom he motioned for me to come up to his desk. Without saying a word he handed me a pink piece of paper and then pointed at the door, basically telling me to leave and go to the main office. He then continued to write something in his notebook, ignoring me while I tried to explain why I was late. Finally he looked up at me and said, "I don't care why you're late. You're wasting my time…go to the main office."

My science teacher was completely the opposite. She took the time to talk to me when I did something wrong. She had short blonde hair and a little hump in her back. She smiled a lot. After being late one day to her class, she walked me out into the hallway and kindly asked me why I was late. I told her that my alarm clock didn't go off. She stared into my eyes and said, "Jaz, you have a lot of potential. I need you to be on time for my class. Next time I will have to send you to the main office and you'll get detention."

I did everything in my power to never be late to the science teacher's class again, although I continued to have issues with the social studies teacher. His action expressed that he didn't care, so I didn't either. Subconsciously I was never in a rush to get to his class again.

When we feel threatened in a relationship, as if our spouse purposely aimed to hurt us, we sometimes rebel by confronting them with anger or avoidance. When I used to fight a lot, I convinced myself that being tough was displayed by responding with anger. Later in life, I realized that being tough was responding with consideration. I'm now able to convey that I'm hurt or disappointed without degrading or yelling at someone. I'm also now mature enough to seek a solution that doesn't end with arguing or separating.

Again, I believe that the key to any successful relationship is professional counseling. Many people will argue that it's too expensive, but just like with anything, there are many affordable options. You just have to have an open mind and look for them. Avoiding an issue is like being sick…in most cases it will not just go away.

Love is a taught behavior. Most people think that it's just given. Like learning how to paint, you have to consistently educate yourself on how to love. This includes loving your friends, family, and most of all. yourself! My past didn't include a lot of preparation and education on how to love…at least the right way! Given my history with sexual abuse, at times love was a murky space in my mind, because of how I had been abused by people I thought loved me.

Although my mother had a huge heart, her rage was an emotion that I would later be attracted to in a woman, so to participate in the art of arguing meant you loved me. After my mother yelled or whipped me she wouldn't verbally apologize, but she'd nonverbally express her sorrow by buying me something. This is how I treated women. I was attracted to the skill of arguing then making up! It's a destructive habit passed down from generation to generation. Now I understand that you have to become the right person to attract the right person.

CHAPTER II

TRYING TO STOP FIGHTING

I argued with women, but I fought with men. I have been in over 200 physical fights. I am humbled by the realization that I'm not in jail, don't have a criminal record, and most amazingly, I am alive. I have come to believe that I was spared, because God has work for me to do.

At a young age my father was also considered a fighter. Years later, as an adult, I realized he was actually a bully. In elementary school I thought I was a hero, because I use to let so-called "nerds" pay me to protect them. That's how I raised money for lunch.

It wasn't until I was about twenty seven years old and I was having a conversation with some close friends I'd grown up with that I realized I had also been a bully as a kid. My friends were making jokes about some of the fights I got into. I looked over at my friend Otis and said, "You never talk about your fights. Did you get into a lot of them?"

Otis was from North Avenue, a part of The Falls considered to be rough, maybe even more horrid than the area I grew up in.

"Jaz, I never fought." Otis said. I stared in shock, "What do you mean you never fought?"

"Jaz, fighting is a choice. You chose to fight," he said. "Actually, I got into one fight. I was in elementary school, arguing with a boy in the courtyard. We weren't going to really fight, but another boy approached us, looked us both in the eyes, slapped me, and said, 'That's from him,' pointing to the guy I was arguing with, then he slapped the other guy and said, 'That's from him,' pointing to me. I went to hit the instigator back and he slammed me. He was on top of me, getting ready to hit me, when the principal approached us. 'What's going on?' he asked. The boy who had been on top of me had the nerve to say, 'We were just playing.' That boy was you."

We started to reminisce about other fights I'd gotten into. A few of us from The Falls went up to a small city called Lockport to meet girls. As a teenager, a new batch of women who it seemed no one was aware of was like striking gold. Everyone knew each other in The Falls. When you got involved with one female, it was almost a given that you were going to have an altercation with her ex-boyfriend. Not a lot of adults from The Falls bothered with Lockport residents, except to visit family and friends in jail. Guys from Lockport were very territorial and didn't want us there.

It didn't take long before the ex-boyfriends in Lockport began to surface. I was about seventeen years old when I dated my first girlfriend from there. My friends and I were chillin' at a young woman's house on a beautiful summer day. She stayed in an apartment development called Sweetwood. Her mother was a drug addict and she normally wasn't home. While my friends and two of her friends played cards in the kitchen, Aisha and I relaxed in the living room talking about the trials of life. A young Mexican guy walked through the front door. I looked at Aisha.

"People don't knock around here?" I asked. Aisha looked at me as if to say, "Do you live here?" then she jumped up and greeted the young Mexican.

"How are you, José?" He stopped in front of the sofa and looked down at me for a moment before responding. "I'm good! What are you up to?"

Aisha told him our names and stated that we were all just hanging out. José appeared nervous and quickly said he had to go. I read the signs: he was going to tell someone, probably an ex-boyfriend, that we were there.

"Tom! Rashaad! It's time to go!" I yelled.

"Jaz, why are you being so paranoid? Calm down. That's just my neighbor. He's harmless," Aisha teased.

"I'm not worried about him. He was clearly uncomfortable with us being here and anxious to leave. I watched him out the window. He ran up a hill as if he was going to rat on us. Plus the bus is coming soon. We have to go!"

I wasn't scared. It was an act. I was curious to know what the young Mexican was up to. After walking outside, I pleaded with Tom and Rashaad, "Let's take the long way to the bus stop. Let's walk up this hill." It was my rage; it could smell a fight from a mile away. The young Mexican was short, very skinny, and wore glasses. He was going to tell a bully, who was more than likely Aisha's ex-boyfriend, that I was here. I read the signs, because I was a bully. So called "nerds" used to provide me with information in return for a false friendship or protection. I was attracted to violence, superiority, and unleashing my rage. I felt there was a bully on top of that hill and, like a lion, I wanted to walk into his backyard and mark it as my territory!

Once we got to the top of the hill I looked around and noticed José across the parking lot talking to a guy in his early 20s who looked Jamaican. Tom stood in front of me and put his hand on my chest and said, "What's going on, Jaz? You got that look in your eyes?"

"I'm good! Let's cut across the parking lot and walk up Sweetwood Drive to get to the bus stop," I insisted. The detour led straight to José. By the time we got to the middle of the parking lot, a young girl ran up to us, "Jaz, how are you?" she said.

I recognized her from an all-night skating event we went to a couple of weeks earlier. "I'm good. How are you?" I said.

She had to be about 13 years old. "You need to get out of here. My brother doesn't have any sense. He's still in love with Aisha," she said.

As she talked, I watched her brother, the Jamaican, go into his apartment. By the way he looked up at me before he went in, I detected something was about to go down. As we continued across the parking lot I asked Rashaad to hide on the side of the building where the Jamaican entered. Tom and I continued to walk across the parking lot with a slow and cautious stride. Seconds later the young man came back outside with no shirt on and a baseball bat in his hand.

"Stay away from here, you little punks," he hollered.

"Who's going to stop us? You and your little bat?" I said sarcastically.

I watched Rashaad pick up a rock on the side of the building. He was behind the Jamaican and out of his sight. As the Jamaican walked aggressively toward us, Rashaad ran up and struck him with the rock. The Jamaican turned around and charged after Rashaad. Immediately Tom and I rushed him from behind. After one or two punches to the head, the Jamaican was on the ground trying to guard his face. We kicked and punched him until I heard a voice yell, "Jaz, get out of here! Someone called the police!"

We all took off running. No one got arrested that night, but I had been arrested many times in Lockport. About six months later I was in a taxi in Lockport and the taxi driver stated, "It's rumored there's going to be a big gang fight out near the mall tonight. You guys might want to stay clear of that area. Every cop in Lockport is supposed to be around there."

I perceived that as a warning sign to stay away from that area and avoid any type of confrontation, but I was hardheaded. Tom and I hung out at Aisha's place until night fall. We walked 15 minutes toward the mall where about twenty of our friends from The Falls greeted us.

"Do you think they're going to show up?" a friend named James asked.

"They'll come! They won't be out here too late, because the cops expect us to meet during mall hours," I replied.

"I'm looking forward to this," my cousin Biggie said.

"I can't stand these young so-called thugs up here. In the meantime, we're going around the corner to Lockport High School. There's going to be a lot of bitches there. It's a major basketball game tonight," James said.

Tom and I decided to walk around to the mall with Aisha and her friend. About an hour later we noticed at least five Lockport boys coming through the main entrance. We were sitting on a bench near the center of the mall. The five boys walked up to us and two of them sat on the bench near us.

"What's up, Jaz?" one of them said as he reached out for my hand.

"Not a whole bunch," I replied. I had seen him a few times around The Falls, but he was from Lockport. He had to be in his early 20s, older than most of us and his counterparts. I hesitated for a moment, but then shook his hand. We talked about clubs, sports, and women. "So what's going on tonight?" the guy asked.

"Nothing. Just chillin," I said.

"Jaz, we know why you're up here. You should just leave it alone. There are at least thirty guys coming out here later just for you," he said.

"I'm not going anywhere! The last thing I'll do is run from a bunch of so-called thugs!" I yelled.

The guy stood up and paced back and forth a couple of times.

"Jaz, you beat a guy named Tony a few weeks ago. His brother was just released from the Marines and wants you badly. He'll be out here soon."

I stood up and got loud, "I don't care if he's a member of G.I. Joe. I don't run from no one, including you and your friends."

"Jaz, you know I'm from Lockport. I don't want to have to hurt no one tonight," he said, just as loud.

"Bring it on. We'll be outside," I said while walking toward the main entrance.

I was just inside a small hallway that led outside when I looked back to see a black man in his 20s and a woman with a long, brown, curly weave walking toward us from an old, brown, Pinto station wagon. It had to be Tony's brother Billie. His eyes were full of rage. I saw the five Lockport guys walking toward us from inside the mall.

Billie yelled from about 30 feet away, "You're going to pay for what you did to my baby brother!"

Without saying a word I ran straight for Billie, but things didn't go as planned, because seconds later I was on my back with Billie on top of me holding me down, then all of a sudden I was being kicked by a bunch of people.

I could hear Tom yelling, "Get off of him!" Then he opened a hole in the crowd big enough for me to sneak through. I got to my feet and ran as fast as I could.

"Follow me, cousin!" I yelled to Tom.

I ran through a couple of apartment developments, a small football field, and then a door at Lockport High School. I slowed down and followed the noise of people cheering. I approached a table with a young woman sitting at it. She looked up at me and immediately said, "two dollars please." I ignored her, walked through the two opened doors, onto the basketball court, looked around, and spotted all my friends from The Falls.

"Biggie, James…come on!" I screamed, pointing to a group of guys. Immediately, at least ten guys leaped down from the stands. They ran with attitude, because they knew something was about to go down. By then Tom came running from behind.

"Who all drove?" I asked, still out of breath.

We left in three cars and headed back to the Lockport Mall. At least five guys were standing in front of the mall engaging in what seemed to be an agitated conversation. Biggie hopped out the car and just started hitting one of them. Soon afterwards we were all surrounding them.

"Now what?" I yelled, as I ran toward one of them, swinging.

After hitting my guy repeatedly, I looked to the left and saw Billie fighting Tom. I ran to join Tom, but by then Billie had managed to get loose. I pulled off my shirt, looked him in the eye, and said, "Just me and you!"

Billie obviously wasn't scared by the look in his eyes, but he was smart enough to back off considering how outnumbered they were. He looked around, assessing the situation, and then yelled, "Let's get out of here." They all ran off through the parking lot.

We chased them across the street. I noticed one of the guys named Puff enter Wendy's. I walked inside and saw Puff at the counter ordering food. I ran in, leaped over the rail, grabbed Puff, picked him up with a hand between his legs and the other hand on his shoulder, and threw him across the room. I leaped back over the rail, got on my knees over him, and began hitting Puff with everything I had. Seconds later I felt a hand grab my shirt near my shoulder, lift me up, throw me against the rails, and punch me repeatedly. When I was able to get up I saw that it was a woman. A couple of women I knew grabbed my attacker and held her against the wall. Later on I found out that it was Puff's mother who attacked me. She worked at the Wendy's. I will never forget the strength a mother musters when protecting her child. I ran out of Wendy's to find all my friends laughing and talking across the street. A woman named Jennifer approached me.

"Jaz, are you alright?" she asked. "Why don't you and your friends come by my place and rest for a minute?" We all were familiar with Jennifer. Even though she lived in Lockport, she was loyal to taking care of me and my friends. I think she had a crush on one of us.

Tom, Michael, and I followed Jennifer down a short street that led to another apartment development. The other guys in the group got into their cars and headed back to The Falls.

Jennifer was accompanied by a short and innocent-looking girl name Tiffany. Once in a while, Tiffany and I talked on the phone, but we'd actually met only once prior to that night. "How are you getting home?" Tiffany asked.

We had actually planned to "jump a cab" back to The Falls, but I wasn't going to tell her that. "Jumping a cab" basically entailed telling the taxi driver that we would pay him when we got to our destination, but once we arrived, we ran, cut through a few buildings, and hid.

The truth was, none of us had enough money to catch a cab back to The Falls, and now that we had let everyone who had driven leave, we had to get home the best way we could. We "jumped a cab" a few times prior to that night. Jennifer suggested that we all stay in Lockport at her house since her parents were out of town. However, Tiffany said I could stay at her place. Tiffany and I headed back toward Lockport Mall to use a pay phone. We walked into a department store called Hills, got something to drink, and then headed toward the phone to call a taxi to get to Tiffany's grandparents.

Tiffany grabbed my hand and said, "I'm going to have to sneak you in my grandparents' house, OK? They'll be sleep."

I was shocked and somewhat nervous. Still I said, "Let's do it."

There were two entrances to Hills which was on both ends of the café area. We waited for the cab, standing in the center of the café area. We were talking when all of a sudden at least twenty or thirty guys swarmed the area, flooded in from both sides of the café area. I recognized a few faces. It was the Lockport crew coming after me!

I told Tiffany to call the police. I ran to the nearest shopping cart, picked it up, and threw it toward the closet people to me, then I turned and ran deep inside the store. I ran toward the sports' section hoping I could find a weapon. I grabbed a baseball bat and began to swing. The next thing I remember, I was sitting in the back of a police car next to Tiffany.

"What happened?" I asked.

Tiffany looked at me with relief and said, "I think you blacked out. Do you remember anything?"

I explained to her and the cop that I only remembered up to the point of picking up the bat. That was the first and only time in my life I had blacked out. Although I had no evident bruises, Tiffany told me that one of the guys hit me with something. She wasn't sure with what.

I believe we were in the police car for about fifteen minutes. The officer took a few notes, told us to stay close by a phone in case he had any further questions, and then let us go. We walked up to a pay phone and called a taxi. After arriving at Tiffany's grandparents' home she told me to wait a minute while she made sure the coast was clear. A couple of minutes later she came back to the door and told me to be quiet while she sneaked me to her bedroom. I sat on the bed and tried to remember what happened. Tiffany walked out the room and returned with a phone.

"Biggie wants to talk to you," she said.

The voice on the other line said, "Jaz, we're going to get them!"

I was still slightly dazed, but Tiffany caressed me and held me as if I were her child. That night we had sex for the first time.

The next morning I called Anthony and asked him to come and pick me up.

"I'll need a couple dollars for gas," he said.

Roughly forty five minutes after we spoke, I peeped out of Tiffany's bedroom curtains, and saw Anthony sitting out front in a teal-green Ford Escort.

Tiffany said, "My grandparents are in the living room. How are we going to get you out of here?"

I looked out the window again. We were on the second floor, directly above the garage. I hesitated and then said, "I'm going to have to jump out the window. It's not that high!" I gave Tiffany a kiss and hug, said thanks, and gently opened the window. I put my legs out first and inched out the window until I was hanging with only my hands holding on to the ledge. I let go and hit the ground a little off balance. I got into the car to witness Anthony laughing so hard that tears streamed from his eyes.

That Friday I got a strange call at my grandparents' apartment. The deep voice said, "I'll be at Club Exit this weekend. I'm coming by myself, and I'm coming for you." It was Billie!

It was unusual for someone to choose to fight with me at Club Exit, considering the club was always full of my friends and family members, but I learned later that Billie wasn't usual. Later on that night, I heard a knock at the door.

"Who is it?" I yelled?

"Nigga, it's Tom. Open the door."

"Man, you're lucky my grandparents didn't hear you," I said as I welcomed him in.

"Nigga, I knew they weren't here," he said. "Their car isn't outside. Are you ready to go?"

"Yep, let's get out of here before my grandparents get home and lecture me about getting into trouble with you," I said cynically.

We walked out the old, hollow, brown door and down the one flight of steps that led to another door that was gray and made of steel. My grandparents lived in the 'hood as well, although it wasn't as bad as other 'hoods around The Falls.

We lived on 12th Street between Buffalo Avenue and East Falls Street. East Falls Street had a lot of crime, mainly dope fiends and drug dealers walked the streets, but they didn't go up 12th Street often. There were a handful of houses on 12th Street and they were occupied by people 60 years old and older. The drug dealers in the neighborhood had a lot of respect for the older people in the 'hood, although the dope fiends had no respect for anyone.

We had to pass an old industrial plant to get to East Falls Street. Many of the dope fiends didn't come up that street, because the plant had a reputation for having mean dogs. Tom and I knew about the dogs and always prepared ourselves as we passed the plant. I went up and down 12th Street most of my life and never knew what they did at that plant. Across the street from the building was a big field that had four to six hills made of 15 feet of broken rock and dirt. As kids, we had played on the hills until the dogs chased us away.

Tom and I both grabbed a stick as we walked by the building. We could have taken a short-cut and followed the railroad tracks over to Memorial Parkway, but we found it entertaining to bypass the old building and listen for the dogs. We walked on the right side of the street, across from the building, which was about 200 feet long. As soon as we got to the end of the building we heard barking. We didn't run, because most of the time the dogs were chained to an old, abandoned tractor, but not every time. Once in a while, the employees wouldn't chain the dogs up. This time the large fence was shut, but had a hole big enough for the dogs to climb through if they had been loose. It was pitch black outside, making the scene gloomy and scary. The dogs barked madly as we walked past. Twenty minutes later we were at the front of Club Exit. There was a long line of people waiting to get in. As we waited, I asked Tom, "Do you have any identification?"

He pulled out an old Medicaid card that had someone else's name on it. We were both 18 years old, just old enough to get in. Because of the warrants he had on him, he couldn't get identification.

"IDs please," the guy at the door demanded.

We both showed the ID we had and walked into the club. It was packed from wall to wall. As we looked for a table, we passed a bunch of friends, shook hands, nodded, and smiled as we made our way through the thick crowd. Halfway through the night I heard a woman scream. I looked to my left and noticed a woman bleeding from the side of her face.

Tom looked to me. "Stay out of it. Reece is trippin'," he said. "He just hit his girl with a bottle."

The bouncers ran over and immediately grabbed Reece and dragged him out of the club. Tom was aware that if we went over there, the bouncers might have mistaken us as instigators, which they normally did. When a fight broke out they usually grabbed anyone who seemed furious and asked questions later.

A few minutes after socializing and mingling, I walked around the club in search of Billie, and fortunately or unfortunately, I spotted him across the room. Tom was on the dance floor entertaining people with his unusual dance moves. I watched a guy bump Tom accidently. Tom turned around, grabbed the guy by his shirt, pulled him off the dance floor, and then returned to the floor as if nothing had happened. I didn't want Tom to see me go after Billie. If Billie was bold enough to come here alone, I had to be bold enough to fight him alone, I thought to myself.

I looked back across the room and spotted Billie coming in my direction. I immediately took off toward him. As soon as I had a clearing and he was about three feet in front of me, I dove through the air and wrestled him to the floor. While on top of him I buckled his arms down with my knees and began to hit him with my fist. Less than a minute into the fight I felt something hard hit me in the back of my head and I heard a loud whack.

I was dazed and confused. Someone grabbed me, picked me up, and threw me onto their shoulder. It was Mark, one of the bouncers. Mark was strong and about three times my size. I tried to shake myself loose but couldn't.

"Put him down, Mark," a voice said from behind.

It was my cousin Jerald. He was about twice my size, but a true Christian who didn't want to hurt anybody, but would when it came to his family. Jerald used to give me all his pass-me-down stuff when we were young. He lived in the suburbs, but I think he always felt sorry for me, because I was raised in the 'hood. His grandmother was like the "godfather" of the family. She was my grandmother's older sister. "I said put him down, Mark," Jerald repeated. Mark put me down and guided me toward a side door that led outside.

Tom ran up to me, "Are you all right?"

"I'm good," I replied.

"No, you're not. You're bleeding all over the place." Tom ushered me to a pizzeria across the street that everyone went to when the club closed.

"Wait right here," he said, running inside and returning with a bunch of napkins. "Put these on your head," he instructed.

I felt blood racing down the back of my neck. It was coming from a deep wound about three inches long on the back of my head. We walked back toward the club. Tom noticed two girls walking through the parking lot. "That's the girl who hit you in the club while you were on top of Billie," he said.

Tom ran off, picked up an old liquor bottle, rushed up to a white girl, and struck her in the stomach. "Bitch, that's for hitting my cousin!" he yelled as the white girl grabbed her stomach in pain. I ran up next and pushed her to the ground. She quickly curled up while holding her stomach and began to cry. "It wasn't me!" she screamed.

I thought to myself, What did I just do!

Tom took off running toward the front of the club. I was still looking at the crying girl in shame. It turned out Tom was running after Billie who stood in the middle of the street motioning Tom to come on. Tom jumped in the air and lunged at Billie. I ran over to help. By the time I got to them they were wrestling on the sidewalk. I reached into my pocket and grabbed my keys. Attached to my keys was a small steel bar, the shape of the letter "F." The bar fit into my fist with two sharp points sticking out between two of my fingers. I pushed Tom aside and started hitting Billie in the top of his head. Blood gushed and ran down his face. I put at least two holes in his head using the steel bar.

My cousin Jerald appeared again, grabbed Billie, and threw him back into the street. "Get out of here, Jaz," he commanded. "The cops are coming."

Three cop cars came from out of nowhere. One of the cops ran up to Billie, but Billie was starting after me once more. The cop grabbed him and demanded that he calm down. Billie wrestled the cop, swinging as if he was possessed. Two other cops ran over to assist with putting Billie into a police car. Tom and I ran down the street.

The following weekend I received another strange phone call. It was my friend Maneo who lived a couple of doors down from my grandmother. Maneo stayed in a worn-out building that his grandparents owned. I lived upstairs from my grandmother.

"Jaz, these two guys came up to my job and jumped me," Maneo said. "They told me to tell you to meet them at 5 o'clock on the corner of Hyde Park Boulevard and Center Avenue. Maneo traveled to Lockport with us every once in a while. He stressed that he had our backs when it came to fighting; but we knew he didn't. Maneo was a lover, not a fighter. He went with us because he was into the women in Lockport. Maneo was very light skinned with bangs and curly hair (Jheri Curl) that went down to his shoulder. Keep in mind, this was about five or six years after the Jheri Curl era faded away. You would think one of his parents was white, but both were African-American. His parents were unique, because they were still together, which in the 'hood, was rare. Maneo would show up at my apartment with a liquor bottle in one hand and a beer in another at 10 o'clock in the morning.

I made a couple of phone calls and waited for Anthony to come and pick me up. Around 4:45 PM we were heading toward Center Avenue when Tom pulled out a small gun. It was a BB gun.

"What are we gonna do with that?" I asked.

"Mom's been in the basement washing clothes and I couldn't go down there to get my real gun, so I stole my brother's BB gun. I'm going to walk up to Billie and shoot him in his eye with this," Tom said.

It was me, Tom, and Anthony in the car. We pulled up to the corner and parked in front of a small apartment duplex. Soon after, Jerald and his friends pulled up. Within about five minutes, there were 15 of us standing on the corner looking around.

"I just want Jaz!" a voice screamed from behind a door a couple of buildings down. Billie walked out and stood in the front yard.

I hesitated, but then said, "Tom, come with me!"

Tom and I walked into the middle of the street. I looked back and saw everyone else following about 10 feet behind—except Reece who was sitting on the curb eating something. I reached into my pocket and grabbed the steel object again. By then Tom and I were 30 feet away from Billie. He looked at my hand and ran back into the apartment. Another guy appeared at the door. He looked familiar. He was light-skinned, short, round, and had a low haircut. I realized he was from The Falls. I also noticed he had a small rifle in his hand.

Bam! The gun fired! Tom and I ran back across the street and hid behind a thick tree. I looked around for the others, but they had disappeared. I saw some of them hiding behind a parked car and others behind trees. I was still scanning the area for all of my friends when a bullet grazed the side of the tree that Tom and I were hiding behind. Bark flew. For some peculiar reason, I wasn't scared. I became impatient, desperate to get to the person who was shooting at me, and punish him. It all seemed surreal, but realizing all of what was actually happening in that moment suddenly made me question my sanity. Without a doubt, I was now sure that I had major issues with anger. Otherwise how could I explain how I had gotten myself into a situation where someone wanted to kill me?

The bark flying around me assured me that this guy was trying to take my life. Something snapped inside of me. I walked boldly from behind the tree and headed toward the door where the gunman stood. Bam! Then it was silent and I saw the gunman run inside. I was about 100 feet from the door. I felt something jerk my body. I stopped in the middle of the street. In the distance I heard people yelling my name. Anthony and Jerald ran up to me. Jerald grabbed me and said, "Jaz, you're shot! You're shot, man! Let's get you to the hospital!"

I looked down at my right arm and witnessed a stream of blood coming from a small hole just under my bicep. A bullet had passed through the center of my arm and exited near my elbow.

I started screaming, "Come out, Billie! I can beat you with one arm! You're dead!"

Anthony walked up to me and demanded that I calm down. I kept screaming. The guys escorted me around the corner as I screamed. A few minutes later I heard sirens.

"We need to get out of here!" I yelled.

Jerald looked into my eyes and said, "Relax, Jaz, it's just an ambulance. Let them take you to the hospital. You don't know what kind of damage that bullet did."

Although I didn't like going to the hospital, I realized that Jerald wanted the best for me and it was time to calm down and pray that I was all right.

I got to the local hospital in approximately ten minutes. A doctor ran up to me and asked me a bunch of questions. They rushed me into the x-ray room. After they took several x-rays I was wheeled to another room and told to wait while they looked over the results.

A different doctor came into my room with a clipboard and said, "There's not much we can do. The bullet passed through your right arm and missed damaging anything major, although it did slightly graze a bone. We saw small fragments of bone, but I wouldn't recommend operating. There is only a small possibility that the small fragments will affect you later in life. If so, then you should have an operation and have them taken out. Be patient for a while. We want to monitor you just to be sure you don't have any difficulties."

Minutes after the doctor left, a police officer entered the room. He asked me a series of questions. I never brought up Billie's name, but I told him the name of the shooter. I wanted him to face two vital consequences: jail and me! When the police officer left I began to pray. I realized that the bullet was less than half a foot from piercing my heart. That moment was the first time I felt God speak back to me. There was no doubt it was God. The voice was strong and demanding and there wasn't anyone else in the room! It was as if He was saying that He spared me and now I would have to spare the guy who shot me. That didn't really sit well with me seeing as how vengeful and eager I was to get both Billie and the shooter for trying to take my life.

In the end, the guy who shot me, Jimmy, did minimal jail time for shooting me, about a year, but it took them a year to catch up with him. He only got caught because he was selling drugs. That's how it is in the 'hood: no one is in a rush to convict thugs that hurt or kill other thugs.

I never went after the guy who shot me. Eighteen months later, after I was arrested for another fight, I saw him in jail. I did about four days before having to go to court and then I was released. During those four days, fellow inmates told me to be careful. Some of them even recommended that I not go outside for recreation, because my charge was so petty and a fight with him would keep me in there for a longer period of time. Others tried to hype me up, suggesting that I beat him down. The first three days I avoided going out to the basketball court. On the fourth day I changed my mind. I wanted him so bad that I didn't care if I got additional jail time for fighting. A couple of correctional officers escorted a small group of us to the basketball court and two fellow inmates reminded me that they had my back. As we walked onto the court I noticed Jimmy talking to a couple of inmates on the other side. Accompanied by my two inmates, I walked toward him. Jimmy looked up at me and began to walk toward me, too.

Within ten feet of each other Jimmy pleaded, "Jaz, I'm sorry. I didn't mean to actually shoot you. I just wanted to scare you. I had been using crack for a while, and let's just say, I wasn't in my right mind that day. I'm going to change my life around."

I reached out my hand, he did the same. We shook hands and walked away. I learned to forgive that day. The fight that would mark the end of my excessive battles and the beginning of a new life made the Buffalo newspaper, nicknaming me "The Frying Pan Bandit."

I was 25 years old and dating a girl named Stephone who I met when I was a computer technician with the Board of Education. We had our first conversation at one of our quarterly meetings for the company. We were all assigned a specific school to review. She told me that her daughter went to the school I worked for and they lived across the street from the school. I asked her to stop by and visit one day and she did. We talked for about a half an hour during my lunch break. I remember she had on a fitted cap, tight blue jeans that exposed her full-sized hips, and a blue jean jacket.

She left me her number and I called her several days later. We dated for a while and it became apparent to our friends and family that we liked each other. Everybody wasn't happy about us dating; she had a child by a Stanto. The Stantos were Italians around The Falls that didn't mingle with black folks much. Although a lot of blacks worked for Italians, it was forbidden to date them, but there were exceptions to the game and Stephone was one.

My former experience with Italians had been memorable. I worked for a few Italians beginning around the age of 16 and they put up with a lot of my immature actions. They owned a local pizzeria and design shop. I had been a busboy at this pizzeria for three years and late one Friday night, a bunch of

Canadian cops were having pizza and beer in the restaurant. I was nineteen years old. I was told to clear the tables and prepare to close. I approached one of the wooden circular tables where the five men sat. I reached for the empty bottles and immediately a man shouted, "We're not done yet!"

"We're closing," I said. "I'm only taking the empty bottles."

The man stood up, looked down at me, and yelled, "Get away from this table! I told you we weren't done yet. Can you hear, nigger?"

I had no tolerance for the N-word. Composed, I backed away from him and headed for the kitchen. Tom was at the sink cleaning dishes. I reached for a knife among the dirty dishes.

Tom grabbed my arm. "You got that look in your eyes. What's wrong?"

I shrugged and moved away from him, heading back to the front. Tom followed me, demanding that I tell him what was wrong.

I walked up to the table, put the knife near the officer's hip and dared him to call me a nigger again. "Let's see how tough you are now. Call me a nigger again?" I taunted. It had seemed that the officer was drunk, but he sobered up when he saw the knife. He didn't say a word.

Tom grabbed me and pulled me back into the kitchen. Minutes later the manager approached me and demanded that I come to the front.

"Did you pull a knife out on this customer?" she asked.

I stood immobile for a second. I couldn't afford to lose this job, so I answered, "No."

Other officers were dragging the drunken one out of the restaurant, because by then he was yelling and calling me names.

The manager looked at me and said, "You're fired."

As I returned to go to the back, one of the owners walked in.

"What's wrong?" he asked. Before I answered, he added, "Wait in the back while I straighten everything out."

Most of the cops couldn't see the knife, because I purposely hung it low, out of the sight of everyone, but the one I threatened. L.A., as they called the owner, returned after about twenty minutes and told me not to worry about anything.

"You're not fired," he said.

That wasn't the first time, or the last time that L.A. looked out for me. Like I said, some Italians were cool, but some didn't like black folks.

So here I was dating Stephone who had a young daughter by a Stanto and the Stantos ran the city. Some were police officers, some were lawyers, and many owned a lot of the local small businesses, like bakeries and restaurants. One Stanto was the Superintendent of the Board of Education, the person my boss answered to.

Rumors started to soar that Mike Stanto, Stephone's daughter's father was after me. He didn't like the fact that a black man was around his daughter. My best friend Brian pulled me aside and tried to convince me to leave Stephone alone.

"Look, Jaz, we all know you can be stubborn and you are obsessed with fighting," Brian said. "Don't fight Mike Stanto! If you do, you won't have anyone to help you considering most of the lawyers wouldn't touch your case. He's a Stanto. The cops will harass you and most of all: you can lose your job, because of who his uncle is. He's a cocky white boy who won't back down to you."

That conversation bothered me. Was I at the bottom of the ladder in social class? Did I have to stop dating a woman because her ex-boyfriend's family had power? Also, I wasn't used to white boys threatening me. I thought to myself, I'm going to get him! I vowed to myself not to let anyone know I was going after Mike, because I didn't want anybody to try and stop me. I planned on outsmarting everyone involved. I had to first wait for the right time. I got a call from Stephone one evening. She was really upset. "Mike attacked me," she cried.

I paused for a moment. "Call the police," I said.

Stephone called me back to say the police had just left. She said that the cop told Mike he couldn't come around until they handled visitation rights in court.

Stephone liked to go to the clubs on Saturday nights so she allowed Mike to stop by again and get his daughter one Saturday morning. I asked Stephone if I could stay that Friday night. When I kissed her that evening, I felt as if I was kissing her for the last time.

Saturday morning we woke up to a loud bang at the kitchen door. Stephone jumped up and yelled to her daughter to get dressed. I unassumingly waited for the signal to get up. Mike knew I was there, because I purposely left my car in front of Stephone's apartment.

He yelled, "I can't believe you got my daughter in there with a nigger!" I jumped up, put on my pants, laced up my shoes, and decided to leave my shirt off.

Mike was still at the door screaming at the top of his lungs, "You whore! Where is the nigger? I know he hears me."

I walked into the kitchen. "Stephone, please take your daughter into the room while I talk to Mike."

I walked up to Mike, gazed into his eyes, and then looked to the left, reached for the chain that locks the door, and pulled it out of the wall.

Mike laughed. "Am I supposed to be scared because you pulled a chain off the wall? Do you know who I am? You're a low-life nigger!"

I backed away methodically, grabbed Stephone's glass coffee pot, and threw it on the kitchen floor. It shattered. I looked at him and he had a devilish smirk on his face. I grabbed a frying pan off the stove and struck him in the head with it. He fell into a corner in the kitchen and I struck him again and again, at least five times, until the pan broke and I only had the handle in my hand.

He looked up at me and smiled again. "That's all you got, you nigger?"

I stabbed him with the frying pan handle piercing the top of his forehead. Blood poured out the top right corner of his head. I struck him repeatedly, focusing on the same spot.

After striking him about six times with the handle, I backed away. I walked over to the old-fashioned telephone that hung from the kitchen wall and called the police.

"Someone has trespassed at a friend's house and he's attacking me," I said. I hung up the phone and by then, Mike was back on his feet, screaming, as if I had no effect on him.

This time I tackled him and we both crashed through the bedroom door where Stephone and her daughter immediately screamed. We landed on the small bed. I continued to strike him with my fist, still focusing on the same spot. Blood was everywhere. As I hit him, I remembered looking up at his daughter, who stared in shock. I stood up, grabbed him by his shirt, dragged him to the back door, pushed him into the hallway, and slammed the door shut. Mike screamed and called me every name in the book from the other side of the door. He walked around to the front porch and looked in the front window at me, still calling me names. I wanted to reach out and pull him through the glass, but that would spoil my plan.

Moments later, the police arrived. Mike was still on the front porch. The first cop ran to him and seemed to be consoling him. Then another police car pulled up. It was the officer from the school where I worked. The first cop on the scene told me that he was taking me to jail after debating back and forth between me, Mike, and them. The woman officer looked at me with sympathy and promised that she would get to the bottom of everything. They eventually took me off to jail. I sat in the jail cell for over an hour before the male cop pulled up a chair in front of my cell. "Tell me the story again," he demanded. ten minutes later, he said they had to let me go.

I returned to work the following Monday. I went to my office and nervously waited to hear from my boss. I didn't doubt that she had heard about the fight, especially since the Buffalo newspaper had an article calling me "The Frying Pan Bandit." It didn't take long. The phone rang. It was the principal's secretary. "Mrs. McKenna would like to see you right away," she said. Mrs. McKenna had been in the newspaper a few months earlier, because her son was caught sleeping on the curb after using drugs. I had seen how dealing with her son's drug abuse had transformed her into a softer person. The principal treated me like one of her children. She was an older, stylish, white woman with short red hair. When I walked into her office she told me to shut the door and sit down.

"What the hell happened?" she asked.

I explained the whole story, leaving out certain details. I talked to her like a young girl pleading to her mother for help. I even started crying a little. She told me that the female cop called her and stated it wasn't my fault. We talked a while and she let me know that I was not going to lose my job if she had anything to do with it.

A couple of days later I was called to meet my boss at the Board of Education. Spike was a hot-headed, young white man. I walked into his office and he started screaming. The superintendent, Starmen Stanto, had called him and told him about the situation. He yelled at me for a few minutes, telling me how embarrassed he was and so on.

"You're fired," he said.

As I got up to walk out his office, his phone rang. I walked unhurriedly, because I suspected it was Mrs. McKenna. I told her before I left the school that I had been summoned to the Board of Education. I was almost at the elevators when Spike called me back into his office.

"Mrs. McKenna really likes you," he said, speaking loudly. "I'm going to take one more chance with you. You're on probation. You can return to work next week."

Of course Mike had filed charges. I was charged with assault and battery. A couple of months later I sat in the hallway of the courtroom watching the jury go in. The jury of my peers consisted mostly of older white males around 40 or 50 years old. I didn't hire a lawyer, because I didn't have money for one, plus I was sure I didn't need one. Anyway, none of the local lawyers would go up against the Stantos. Already looking defeated, my public defender requested that I follow him to the judge's chambers. I walked into a luxurious office to see an old white man in a long, black robe, obviously the judge, sitting behind a cherry wood desk. He was looking down at a set of papers, one hand on his forehead and the other holding onto a pen he was tapping on his desk; he looked up at me in disgust.

"You don't have to go in front of the jury, you're a free man," the judge said. "But, young man, I know what you did. If I ever see you in my courtroom again, I'm going to throw the book at you."

I walked back out to the hallway, sat in a chair, and put my head down. Someone tapped me on the back. I looked up to see one of my cousins.

"You got away with it again, huh?" he asked.

I was still in disbelief. I set up the whole situation. The case was thrown out, because Mike Stanto had been told that he could not return to Stephone's apartment until after they went to Family Court. I knew that, which is why I told her to call the cops the day they got into an argument. I stayed that Friday night knowing that he was coming over the next morning. I also was aware of the fact that the female cop from the D.A.R.E. program would be on patrol. D.A.R.E. is an international substance abuse prevention education program that seeks to prevent use of controlled drugs, membership in gangs, and violent behavior. I snatched the chain off the door to make it look like he had forced his way into Stephone's home. I slammed the coffee pot onto the floor to show he tried to attack me first. I called the police to express I was the victim. I orchestrated it all, but Mike helped. He was already known to have an explosive temper, so my goal was to attack his character, so his family would sympathize with my actions and not come after me.

I had planned everything and it had worked so beautifully, but even I could see that I had come dangerously close to losing this time. A change had to come, otherwise I was staring at death. I sat in the chair that day and again heard a voice demanding that I stop fighting.

THE TRANSFORMATION

After the Stanto case, I had vowed to never fight again. I was 28 years old and I felt as if God's patience with me was becoming thin. Then this happened.

I was hanging out with my brother at a club called Roxy's in Hamilton, Ontario. I was talking to a distant friend from The Falls named Cornel when I noticed my brother was arguing with someone. Of course I ran over, but my only intention was to calm him down. He was clearly upset, because he was yelling. I had retired from fighting… at least, so I thought.

I suppose the problem with my retirement was that I was the only one who knew I was retired. Everyone else just knew me from my reputation and years of fighting, so before I got an opportunity to be a peacemaker, another guy came out of nowhere and struck me with a beer bottle. I didn't see who did it, but I assumed the guy who hit me was a friend of the guy my brother was arguing with. He probably thought I was going to provoke the situation. I had come full circle.

Blood flowed down my face. I wanted to take action, but I couldn't move. It was as if an invisible, dominant being was holding me. I was conscious. I could see and hear everything around me, even though the heavy blood that dripped down the right side of my face blurred my vision and limited my hearing. It was then that I heard the Voice. It didn't seem to be coming from anyone in the room. The Voice seemed quite upset and was yelling! It had the tone of a father warning his child. I know I was conscious, because I could see everyone around me yelling and screaming, but I could barely hear them. The Voice I heard was aggressive, strong, and unimaginable; it was also frightening, yet I felt protected.

The Voice said things like, "It wasn't you. It was Me that kept you out of trouble. It was Me that kept you from spending the rest of your life in jail. It was Me that kept you from losing fights. It was Me that kept you from death!"

Everyone in the club seemed to be startled and most of them were heading toward the exit. I was in Canada, another country, and like so many battles I'd witnessed in my life, this one came down to territory. The people who came to my aid were mostly from The Falls, New York. The club attracted a lot of people from across the border and we stuck together. I remember Cornel yelling repeatedly, "Let's get 'em, Jaz! I got your back!"

Cornel and a girl name Roxanne escorted me into the kitchen.

"Are you all right, Jaz? Are you all right?" they shouted.

I couldn't answer. I just stood there in shock, still frozen. Not in shock from the blow, but I still felt as if someone or something was yelling at me. I began to reminisce about my past. The Voice showed me parallels of how it spared me. Images laced with storylines of how It helped me avoid jail, and even death, ran through my head.

It was clear to me that I was being shown and told the truth: It was God, not me who got me through 200 or more fights. All this time I thought I had won, because I was just good at what I did. As I stood there, another man was shoved into the kitchen. He was a tall, skinny, white man with a black Roxy's shirt on. He stared at me in shock. He was the guy who hit me. I could tell by the frightened expression on his face. I looked to my left and saw a fork in the sink. I thought to myself: I could make it to that fork and stab him before someone could stop me.

Then I heard the Voice again: "You do it this time and you're on your own. I won't protect you this time."

Roxanne grabbed me and forcefully escorted me out of the kitchen. The club was empty. She accompanied me outside and directed me into her car. My brother followed in my car. She lived only a couple of blocks away.

"Jaz, you need to go to the hospital," she suggested.

"I don't like hospitals. I'm fine," I replied.

We pulled up onto a parking ramp that was connected to a tall building. We got out of her car and entered the elevator and went up to the fifth floor. After walking into her apartment, she immediately ran to the bathroom and returned with a wet towel. As she patted the towel on my open wound, she repeated,

"Jaz, you really need to go to the hospital."

CHAPTER 12

LEARNING TO BE SUBMISSIVE

I returned to The Falls. As soon as I entered my room, I got on my knees and prayed like I had never prayed before. "God, I quit fighting. I know it was You that won those fights, not me. I am ready to follow You. I know You want me to leave The Falls. I am ready to leave. I am willing to leave my family and friends…" I prayed for about 30 minutes. I looked up to see that it was three o'clock in the morning—and my phone rang.

I picked up the phone. "Hello."

"Hi, Jaz, it's Michelle," the soft voice replied. "Do you remember me?"

Of course I remembered her. I had dated Michelle about a year prior to that night. Ironically, we had talked about leaving The Falls one day, but at the time, leaving my hometown was my biggest fear. The Falls was familiar. All of my family and friends were there.

"Of course I remember you," I said.

She went on to say that she was living in The Queen City, North Carolina. "It's challenging—expensive," she said. "I need a roommate."

It was no coincidence that she had called at that very moment. It was a sure sign that it was time for me to leave home!

"I'll be your roommate, but you will have to give me to the end of the summer to raise enough money to leave," I said.

I was off of work for the summer. I was employed by EduTech, a vendor for the Board of Education. My first thought was, how am I going to raise at least a thousand dollars to leave? Strangely, that summer, money started to come in. I helped a close friend with handyman work.

Yet even though I had committed to moving and money was pouring in, I wasn't fully convinced that I was going to leave. I started crossing the Canadian border more often. I began hanging out with a Canadian woman named Megan. I stayed over there for about a week, blowing my money. Subconsciously, the lack of money was going to be my excuse not to leave.

Prior to the incident at Roxy's, I met Megan. Her parents had a huge house. They had a refrigerator full of food, a sound system with speakers in every corner, a lot of alcohol, and a backyard that was bigger than our community park. Every night was like a party, because her parents were on vacation. Even with a refrigerator full of food, we went out to eat every night. Some evenings we went shopping and to the movies. I returned home almost broke, and again, opportunities came up to make extra money. I couldn't spend the money fast enough, but still my excuse for not leaving was going to be I was out of money.

In spite of my bad habits, by the end of the summer I had managed to save about eight hundred dollars. I walked around my apartment, sad and frustrated. What should I take with me? I thought to myself. This was an opportunity to be reborn, to start over, so I decided under those circumstances I didn't need to take much. I figured I might take my bed, which was nothing but two mattresses sitting on the floor, and my raggedy, brown, wood dresser that was missing a few handles, my clothes, my television, and my black entertainment center.

I only needed a small truck to transport the items. I called U-Haul and got a ridiculous quote. They wanted six hundred dollars just to ship a few small items, so now I had another excuse; the truck was too expensive for me to move. After all, I couldn't go down to The Queen City with only two hundred dollars in my pocket…do the math. I called Michelle and told her the bad news. I figured she would be upset, so I tried my best to sound as pathetic as I could. Her reply shocked me.

"How much stuff do you have to move?" she asked. I told her about the few items I'd decided to bring.

"I'll call you right back," she said. A few minutes later, the phone rang.

"Jaz, you won't believe this but my parents are moving down this way as well," Michelle said.

"They got a truck that was bigger than they expected. They have plenty of room to move your stuff."

"When are they planning to move?" I asked.

"Within two weeks," she replied.

All I could say was, "All right, let's do it!"

I hung up the phone in shock. How could this be? I still had a problem: my car was not in any shape to make it to The Queen City, which was 640 miles away. Moments later, the doorbell rang.

"Who is it?" I yelled.

"Open the door," a voice replied.

It was Oscar, one of my close friends who served as a handyman for an apartment development called Unity Park and for other private landlords. He was the person who had hired me over the summer to help with a couple of projects. Of course I told him the story about how Michelle's parents were moving around the same time I was supposed to move. I also mentioned that I still had the dilemma with my car not being in shape to make it to The Queen City.

Oscar said, "I got your back. Let's sell your car. That will give you extra money and you can borrow one of my cars to take to The Queen City."

Oscar had two nice cars, one was a deep black Pontiac Bonneville that I loved driving and the other was a new black Ford Escort.

"You would actually let me borrow one of your cars? For how long?" I asked.

"I'll give you a few months to get on your feet," he said.

At the age of 28 years old, I had become submissive to someone—to God—for the first time in my life. I decided to sincerely leave for The Queen City.

I was at work a couple of weeks prior to leaving for The Queen City when someone told me to turn on the television. I sat in shock, watching a plane as it crashed into a building in New York City. It was September 11, 2001. I was sitting in the computer lab at Niagara Street Elementary School with a senior technician, an older white man who didn't really care for me. However, in that moment, it was like we bonded as we watched what was happening in shock. At first I was in denial. It had to be a clip from a movie, I thought to myself.

The old man looked back at me and said, "This is sad. This is going to affect our country for years to come."

I didn't understand what he was suggesting. I was numb. I just continued to stare at the screen for at least an hour while the news reported the violent and unfortunate incident. I had no idea how this incident would impact my journey to The Queen City. Days before I left, I spent a day with my son DeShaan. He was 8, and not fully aware of what was about to happen. I bought him a couple of toys and a game for his PlayStation out of guilt and hoped that somehow, they would entertain him enough that he wouldn't care that I was leaving.

As we drove from the Lockport Mall and headed toward his grandparents' house, DeShaan sat, silent and dejected. I watched him in the back seat from the rearview mirror. I attempted to spark a conversation, but he just nodded and stared. It was a difficult time, considering I was trying not to get upset myself. I felt like I had to be strong. I also began to question my decision: Was I doing what my father did to me? Was I going to be a bad father for leaving my son? When would I see my son again?

We pulled up into his grandparents' driveway. I paused and put my head on the steering wheel, trying not to cry. I opened my door and walked to the back door and unfastened his seatbelt. I picked him up and carried him to the front door. His arms were wrapped tightly around my neck while his chin rested on my shoulder. I rang the doorbell and after a few seconds, the door opened. I walked in and reluctantly put DeShaan down. He immediately walked away, stopped, and began to cry. It would be one of the hardest things I ever faced in my life. Again I thought: Would God really want me to leave my son? I walked up to DeShaan, picked him up, squeezed him gently and whispered in his ear, "I'm sorry. You might not understand for a long time, but I have to go. I will not give up on you. I love you." Then I put him down and left.

It was a long thirty-minute drive back to The Falls from Lockport. As soon as I arrived home, my phone rang. My cousin Anthony insisted that we all go out. I pleaded and tried to tell him that I wasn't in the mood, but an hour later, Anthony, Otis, Oscar, Ace, Black, and Taiwan arrived at my place. We were all at a club called Pharaoh's in The Falls in less than an hour. The club was packed and surprisingly, a lot of people approached me and wished me luck on my journey to The Queen City.

My Uncle Ken had let me borrow his car that night to get around. After saying goodbye to all my friends, I took off to his house to drop off the car. I lied to him and my Aunt Ellen. I told them that I had a ride from their house back home. I lied, because I wanted to walk, and I knew they wouldn't approve, because it was two o'clock in the morning. After hugging my Aunt Ellen, I walked toward my mother's house, which was about 20 minutes away. A block or so into the walk, my eyes began to water. I felt as if I was going to cry, but all of a sudden it began to rain. To this day, I don't know whether I actually cried or not that night.

I arrived at my mother's soaking wet. I walked up two stories to her bedroom. I watched her for a few moments while she slept. She opened her eyes and smiled. I thought she would try to talk me out of leaving, but instead she said, "You will be all right. You will go down to The Queen City and do great things."

I couldn't help but wonder who would protect her, not realizing at the time that she could protect herself. I lay beside her for a few minutes, gave her a hug, and then called a taxi to take me home.

CHAPTER 13

FROM THUG TO GENTLEMEN

It was a long journey to The Queen City. I followed Michelle's parents in Oscar's car. Even though I was following them, it was my first time driving that far by myself. They drove the U-Haul that contained their furniture and a few of my items, including my bed, my television, my dresser, my desk, my computer, and my clothes in at least ten garbage bags. I sold everything else to my mother's boyfriend, including my kitchen table, my living room set, and my air conditioning unit. I didn't want to take a lot of things with me. I played a song by Beanie Sigel over and over again called "Remember Them Days."

I arrived in The Queen City to find an apartment building that looked like a huge upgrade considering where I'm from. I couldn't help but wonder why Michelle's parents were so willing to let a black man from the ghetto live with their white daughter and their four-year old granddaughter. We got to Michelle's place at about one o'clock in the morning. She opened the door, looking attractive, but tired. I gave her a hug and said "thanks."

I stood at the door and looked around. The walls were clean, the rug appeared brand new, but their furniture was old and worn.

Michelle smiled and said, "It's a big leap from The Falls, huh?" I understood wholeheartedly what she was implying. It was a pleasant way of saying, "It feels good to be out the 'hood, huh?"

I thought back to a line from Beanie Sigel's song: "It's all good now, we out the 'hood now!"

It would be days later before I discovered that Michelle actually lived in a bad part of The Queen City. Still, it was better than what I was used to. I was confident that I could get a job for the Board of Education in The Queen City, but again, I arrived right after 9-11. Most businesses were cutting back, including the Board of Education. Someone told me about another place called Sitel that was hiring computer technicians. I applied for the job and was set up for an interview a few weeks later. I had to take a test on mapping.

I knew nothing about maps. I use to travel a lot as a rap artist, but I was bad with directions, especially navigating on Interstates. When I drove, every time I got off the Interstate to get gas, I had to ask someone which way to get back on the Interstate. I didn't even know what mile markers were or what they were for.

As I attempted to answer each question on the test, the examiner paced back and forth behind me, and occasionally stopped and pointed out the right answer secretly. Yes, he helped me cheat. I was then given a position with the company, although I still had to pass a six-week training class. Throughout the six weeks I was clueless as to what I was getting myself into. The classes consisted of about 20 students. The foundation of the work centered on customer service: how to greet and answer questions from customers who called in from their vehicles. We learned a lot about the technology and how to direct and navigate people while they were driving.

The building I worked in was massive. It had a large cafeteria, a workout facility, and a lot of offices. Within three weeks, we were reassigned to a new training class. In order to get there, I had to pass by an enormous window that had a few hundred people on the other side. They were sitting in little cubicles, each with a computer, and they were wearing headphone devices on their heads. I finally figured out I was working at a call center.

There was another training class that started at the same time we did. Our teacher was cool and gave us a lot of freedom, but the other class was known to have a strict teacher. Once a weekm the instructors combined the classes for certain training exercises. For the most part we all became friends and learned to watch each other's backs. We helped each other on tests, ate together in the cafeteria, and sometimes met after work.

Toward the end of the training period I became cool with a guy named Randolph. He was unconventional. He offered me a partnership in a couple of his ventures, like robbing a trucking company that stored and shipped electronics. He had a new scheme every week. I never agreed to help him with his illegal activities, although I entertained his conversations. I was used to people like Randolph, gangsters, mobsters, thieves, drug dealers…people like that were all comfortable around me. I'm not sure if it was my scars, tattoos, laid-back style, attitude, or just my black skin that made so many people comfortable around me!

Randolph wasn't a bad individual; he was a rich kid that had been taught bad habits. One day, out of nowhere, Randolph decided to play matchmaker. He wanted me to meet a girl from the other training class, so while leaving class for lunch one day, he asked me to follow him down a runway that led to the workout facility where he introduced me to Carol. She looked confident but insecure, happy but sad, beautiful but didn't know it. We ate lunch together for a few weeks, and then started dating. Little did

I know that our relationship would change my life once again and lead me down a road of activism and leadership.

We both passed the training classes and were employed as Subscriber Advisors. Our teacher finally escorted us onto the main floor where a couple hundred people sat. There we each got our own little cubicle with a computer and a headphone device. Again, this was the first time I had known anything about call centers. Call centers didn't exist in The Falls until around the time I was leaving. I was upset. I had a long talk with God that night.

"You brought me this far to work at a call center for ten dollars an hour?" I asked. I prayed, yet deep in my heart I didn't doubt that I was supposed to be in The Queen City. Nevertheless, I couldn't comprehend why I was at a call center. Like most people employed at this call center, I complained a lot the first two years. Negativity was like a disease there. No one wanted to be at the center. The managers complained just as much as the advisors. Actually, there was a small group of seniors, about 50 years old and older, who didn't complain that much, if at all. They just came to work and did their jobs. They only engaged in a conversation with the complainers when we weren't talking negatively, otherwise they just sat at their computers and kept to themselves. I called them "the wise ones."

I got away with a lot at the call center, everything from cussing out managers to being late and taking excessive breaks. Having good street smarts, and understanding how to survive in the corporate world, I perceived what I could get away with and when I could get away with it. When they upgraded the technology that monitored when we went on breaks, I cleverly waited a few weeks until I understood the new system and then I returned to spending more time than allowed away from my computer.

A few months into my employment, I realized why I got an interview so quickly: call centers have a high turnover rate. OnStar/Sitel had over a thousand employees, which equated to many of them being treated like a number. This was why people stayed upset. When one person was caught doing wrong, like coming to work late or eating on the floor (at their desks), the whole team was punished and ridiculed.

Carol and I got along great for the first year. After that, we began to fight, sometimes at work. We didn't fight on the main floor, but we argued in the hallways, the gym, and the cafeteria. This, of course, made our jobs harder and more stressful. I began to wonder if it was the stress of the job that was affecting our relationship. I started to think that if we could find a way to advance to another team it would lessen our stress. There were other teams in the building. One team, the people who handled emergency situations, was upstairs. The emergency team handled people who got into accidents or felt threatened. It was a small team and I soon learned it was hard to get on that team.

One day, Human Resources sent out a posting via email about a new position called Sales Subscriber. They had ten positions available. I asked Carol if she wanted to apply and she said no. Carol didn't like the team she was on, but she was accustomed to it. I kept trying to persuade her, and eventually she agreed to request an interview for the sales team. Being a Communications graduate, I figured I could help her, so I advised her on how to get on the team. I had already gone to Human Resources and inquired about the requirements. In college I learned to ask a teacher what was going to be on a test, because, like a sponge, I'm great at soaking up information and storing it.

We both applied for the Sales Subscriber position, but Carol was called for an interview and I wasn't. I was highly upset. I ran around the call center from manager to manager demanding a chance. Finally, two weeks after Carol's interview I received an email stating that they would interview me for the position. By then Carol was making more money and was ranked number one on the sales team.

To prepare for my interview, I sat up with Carol for two nights quizzing her about the interview she had with them and the details about the job requirements. I was well prepared and confident. Two days after the interview I received an email stating that I was denied the chance to go to the sales team. I didn't understand because they had basically asked me the same questions they asked Carol and I was prepared for each one. I went to Human Resources the next day and asked to know the reason why I was denied. No one gave me a direct answer or sensible reason. They just said, "We'll look into it."

OnStar gave people who bought a brand-new GMC vehicle the basic "Safe & Sound" package free for the first year. It did not include the directional package. The OnStar button, which was located on the rearview visor, was only to be used to speak with a Subscriber if you ran into an emergency situation. Carol's job was to convince new buyers to renew their package after the first year expired and to upgrade to one that included directions. She got a commission for every person she upgraded or renewed. When I saw her first check, I was even more determined to get on the sales team. Human Resources began avoiding me. They couldn't come up with an answer as to why I was not approved. Personally I thought it was because Carol was an attractive female that got her on the sales team.

I was finally approved to go upstairs to sales after about a month of my continuously harassing managers and staff. The next two years I was their number one sales associate. Carol's performance was normally close to mine. For the first time in my life, I was making close to $40,000 a year. As regular Subscribers we made less than $20,000 a year. This was big money for me or anybody from my neighborhood. Uneducated with the knowledge of how to use money smartly, I started taking big trips with my son. I wanted him to see and witness places outside of The Falls and The Queen City. We went to stay in cabins in the mountains and beachfront hotels. We were entertained at major festivals and jaw-dropping amusement parks and more. I felt like I was finally having fun and just loving life! However, the more I made, the more I spent.

As time went on, OnStar began to decrease our commission and increase our workload. A manager showed us a graph that illustrated how much each one of us had made for OnStar for the past year. I was the highest earner; I helped them profit over a million dollars. The graph made me realize that what I had done for OnStar I could possibly do for myself. I also wondered why the more I earned, the more money they took from me. I got upset one day and marched into a manager's office. Jeff was a young white male who was normally calm and good at avoiding answers, like some politicians.

"How can you treat me this way? I bust my ass for this company and all you do is take more and more money away from me and give me more work!" I yelled.

Jeff smugly put his hands behind his head, reclined back in his chair, and said, "You don't have to be here."

"You're…" I paused. I finished the rest of the sentence in my head: You're right. I marched out of his office and headed back to my little desk. For a brief moment I was mad and frustrated, then finally, for the first time, I accepted my role and the reason I was still working for this company. I saw clearly that for the past couple of years, like most of my peers, I had complained and dreaded every moment on the job. That time had ended. My wonderful, terrible job had taught me what I needed to know—and now I was free to go.

CHAPTER 14

BOOKS CHANGED MY LIFE

A day before my short chat with Jeff, a friend named Joe approached me with a book and pleaded with me to promise to read it from front to back. The book was called Feel the Fear and Do It Anyway by Susan Jeffers, Ph.D. I couldn't foresee the influence the book would have on my life, but at the age of 30, it would be the first book I ever read from cover to cover…literally!

In the book Susan (as she likes to be called) encourages her readers to get rid of unconstructive, negative, and doubtful words. She inspires people to embrace the things in life they fear and then overcome them. I didn't know it at the time but Susan Jeffers has helped millions of people throughout the world overcome their fears, heal their relationships, and move forward in life with confidence and love.

Her book encouraged me to stop complaining, face my fears, and become successful. I had been afraid to go after a big dream for fear of failure or affirmation that I wasn't worthy or smart enough. I always surmised that being raised in the 'hood gave me an advantage when it came to problem solving and knowing how to use my street smarts to my advantage. However, having good street smarts can sometimes come with its own disadvantages.

There are times when we think we have won the war, not understanding that the battle has just begun. One disadvantage of trusting only on street smarts occurs when we lack the knowledge to make the right choice. Another disadvantage is not developing the skills to have learned how to effectively stay driven and focused with deep-rooted endurance, passion, love, faith, common sense, and knowledge. The knowledge I'm referring to consists of fundamental skills to deal with everyday issues, like our health, finances, relationships, business, etc. In the 'hood I didn't see a lot of examples in these areas and when I was a student, the education system refused to teach me these traits as well. Susan Jeffers inspired me to know that I can be something great, and I would later use this wisdom to inspire other people to be great, too.

About a week prior to reading Susan's book, I tried to read a book by David Walker, a manager that worked for Sitel as well. David was around fifty five years old and originally from Canada. He came to work with a sincere cheerfulness about himself. We got into a brief debate one day in regards to blacks in the United States. His impression of blacks came from raunchy rap videos, stereotypical sitcoms, and movies on TV. David asked if I would read a book he wrote, and I agreed to read his book. I did what I always did in the past, I skimmed through it, but this time was different. I read information in his book that intrigued me.

Reading David's book would be the closest I ever came to finishing a book in its entirety prior to reading Susan's book. I wasn't illiterate, but never felt the need to read a book from front to back. Even with an Associate's Degree in Communication and Media Arts, I used my photographic memory to get by. I never read the books professors requested that we read.

David's book educated me on Canadian laws and regulations, but he also wrote about his life and coming from a two-parent household, which educated me on different degrees of love.

After skimming through his book, I asked David, "How do you come to this job day after day with a genuine and resilient smile on your face with all the negative energy that flows through this place?"

"It's simple, I just look forward to going home to my best friend, my wife," David said. "Just the thought of her gets me through the day."

Up to that point in my life, I had never heard anyone express such heartfelt love for another person in just two sentences! A friend named Mark approached my desk with another book. Mark was unique as well. Unlike most of us, he came to work with a smile on his face and he was younger than me. Mark put a book in front of me called Who Moved My Cheese? by Spencer Johnson. I glimpsed up at Mark as if to say, "Don't tell me you want me to read a book, too?" But that's exactly what he wanted me to do. Mark insisted that this 94-page book would help transform me into an avid reader. The book's focal point was about change. Like Joe, Mark requested that I promise to read the book from front to back. I agreed since it was only 94 pages.

A remarkable thing happened once I read Spencer's book. I began to embrace change. I realized that I was stubborn and scared of the unknown. When something was taken from me, I preferred to stay in one place and complain rather than look for another opportunity. I invite you to read the previous three sentences again to understand how profoundly my transformation was occurring! All of my reading was sparking new ideas and thoughts, even a new attitude. I was ready to take a big step to change my life. Carol and I had a long conversation one night. We talked about starting a business. I stressed to her that

I wanted to do something that would inspire the urban community to read and then she blurted out, "What about a bookstore?"

"That's it!" I shouted.

It was February of 2004. I prayed long and sincerely one night about the idea of a bookstore and after my prayer, I told Carol that we would open a new bookstore on December 10th, 2004. (Don't forget this date, it'll come up again!)

Mind you, I only owned three books: David Walker's book, Courage of Malice, Susan Jeffers' book, Feel the Fear and Do It Anyway, and Spencer Johnson's book, Who Moved My Cheese? How in the world would we find enough books to fill a bookstore? How would we get the funds to start it? I asked these questions, though I was confident that my purpose had been revealed to me from God and that the pieces would fall into place.

From that point on I no longer joined most of my co-workers in complaining at work, and I replaced every spare moment I had with preparing, researching, and planning to start a bookstore. The call center had hundreds of gifted and talented individuals, so I asked around for advice. One coworker named Michelle left Onstar/Sitel to work as a manager at a Goodwill retail store and a couple of weeks later called to say she had hundreds of books that she could sell me at an affordable price. This exchange developed into a routine. At least once or twice a week Carol and I stopped by the Goodwill and purchased boxes of books. I stored the boxes in my spare bedroom.

By the end of March—between the donations received from friends and the books we purchased—we had over a thousand books. One day while shopping at a Goodwill store near my apartment, I recognized a series of books by one particular author. An older man I occasionally ran into was also browsing through the books.

"Excuse me sir, do you know this author, John Grisham?" I asked. "He seems to have a lot of different titles, so I'm assuming he's a good author."

"Didn't you tell me you were opening a bookstore, young man?" The man responded.

"Yes, I am."

He paused a moment, looked me up and down, and said, "How are you going to open a bookstore and you don't even know who John Grisham is?" He shook his head and continued to look through the various selections of books. I stood in one spot, a little discouraged and humiliated.

That night I sat at my computer for hours looking up popular authors. I also found websites that sold brand-new books called "remainder books" that were very inexpensive. Carol and I were using funds from our paychecks to purchase books, therefore, it was obvious that we needed to find a way to borrow money. A friend, coworker, and mentor named Larry Gaddy told us we needed to create a business plan. He also informed me that The Queen City was a major hub with an assortment of resources and funding for small businesses. He directed us to a community college with a small-business center that would help us.

The next day I made an appointment at the Central Piedmont Community College small business center. Carol and I met with a woman who told us about an organization called S.C.O.R.E. S.C.O.R.E. is a mentoring program with experienced leaders that provide advice to another to help them succeed. She stated that they would help us prepare a proper business proposal at no charge to us. She recommended that we meet with one of their small business counselors. She also told us about a program they had for getting funds. We had to attend a two-hour class before applying for a loan. We took the class, applied—and received a $7,000 loan!

My vision was for more than just a retail bookstore. I wanted to educate people who didn't know how to read and have educational programs that offered reading tutors. I didn't know it at the time, but the programs that offered a way to give back to the community also qualified me to get certain grants. It made perfect spiritual sense — when you broaden your vision to start a business with the intention of helping others, your reward is more resources and opportunities.

Carol and I were grateful to get the $7,000 loan, but we needed more to start the bookstore. I made an appointment with a member of S.C.O.R.E. and met with an elderly white man who was very blunt. He gave me a disc and said, "On this disc are about a hundred questions. You will have to conduct a lot of research to answer most of the questions about the industry you're trying to get in. It will help you design a business plan based on your answers. Come see me after you're done, or if you have any questions putting it together. From there, we'll look into some opportunities for funding."

I stood up, shook his hand, and headed for the door. As I approached the door, I whispered, "I'm going to find and pay a good writer to help me."

The elderly man heard me. "If I find out you paid someone to help you, I will not help you," he said. "It's important that you and your partner do it yourselves, so that you'll know what you're getting yourself into."

Carol and I began to look for someone to help answer the questions and write the business plan once we reviewed the disc. It wasn't because the member of S.C.O.R.E. told me not to, but because I didn't think I could write one! In the meantime, I did some research. I went to a couple of local bookstores and asked questions based on the information provided on the disc.

One day, after stopping by a few bookstores that were hesitant to give me all the information I needed, frustrated and tired, I pulled over to the shoulder of the road and prayed. I still had a bunch of unanswered questions. I went by every bookstore in The Queen City that was listed in the phone book. After praying, I decided to go home. As I began to pull off, I looked to my right and noticed a peculiar brick building. One side seemed to be a church and the other side was a bookstore. I drove into the parking lot and looked around for a door to enter the bookstore. The only door that seemed to be open was one that led to a hallway between the church and the bookstore. I opened another set of doors and walked into a room that led to a health food store. A young black woman sitting behind the counter looked up.

"Can I help you?" she asked.

Looking around and spotting books, I replied, "I'm a student and I'm doing a paper on bookstores. Is a manger available for me to ask a few questions?"

The lady yelled out a name and soon a young white man with dark black hair appeared from around the corner with a broom in his hand. "How can I help you?" he asked.

I lied to the lady behind the counter, because I was afraid she would treat me like the other stores and not try to help someone who was opening another bookstore, but there was something exceptional about this man and I immediately felt guilty about lying, so I told him the truth. He smiled at me, walked toward a nearby bookshelf, and grabbed a hardback book from the bunch.

"I'll make a deal with you. You promise to take this book home and read it, I'll answer any questions you have," he said. "This book is a gift from me to you." The book was entitled The Proverbial Cracker Jack How to Get out of the Box and Become the Prize by Dale Henry. Just as I'd promised David, Joe, and Mark, I agreed to read it, and the man proceeded to answer all of my questions. I headed home and started reading.

It took me a week to finish the book. I had never felt a person's character through a book before. I felt as if the author and I were personally acquainted. The author appeared to be a kind, sincere, and genuine guy dedicated to helping people. Over the next couple of years, I would use that book many times as a reminder on how to embrace the many obstacles I'd face in regards to becoming an entrepreneur. Dale Henry taught me to slow down and enjoy life. He also taught me how to deal with what most people call problems and to redefine them as only inconveniences. I found someone to help with the business proposal, not realizing how much work we had already put into it. I called Carol with the good news.

"Jaz, we're pretty much done. It looks good," she said.

We took our proposal to S.C.O.R.E for their approval. The elderly man agreed that it looked good. "The next step is to get you another loan," he told us.

CHAPTER 15

THE 'HOOD COMES WITH NO CREDIBILITY

I took our proposal to a bank called Wachovia. A young white man greeted me in the main lobby. He told me to follow him into an enclosed office with a lot of windows.

"How can I help you?" the man asked.

I reached into my briefcase and retrieved the business plan. "I'm going to open a bookstore here in The Queen City. I need a loan for $20,000."

The man grabbed the proposal and carefully looked through it. After about a minute, he looked up at me. "You appear to have done your research, although, I don't see the financial statements."

"They're in the back of the proposal," I replied.

Again, he took his time looking through the 22-page proposal. "Do you have any type of collateral?" he asked.

"Yes sir. I have $7,000."

I had already conducted research on some major and minor rules and regulations to getting a loan. One major rule was a person should have at least 25 percent of what they were requesting from the bank. The bank clerk stood up.

"Give me a couple of days to make a decision. We will have to check a couple of things, including your credit score."

I shook his hand and walked out of his office. As I drove off, I thought about my credit score. I wasn't prepared for him to check my personal credit score. Someone had told me that a bank goes off the tax ID of the business, not my personal credit. I had never even had a personal credit card or taken out a loan from a bank with the exception of student loans. Days later, the bank teller called.

"The bank is unable to give you a loan," he said.

"Why?" I asked.

"There is a judgment against you on your credit report," he said.

When I was 21, soon after my son was born, I went back to school. During that time, I lived next door to my grandparents' house, but most of my mail still went to my old address which was upstairs from my grandparents' apartment. My son Deshaan was staying with me on the weekends. One day my grandmother called and told me to come to her place to discuss something important. She showed me a couple of bills from Child Support for $75 a week.

"Why are they sending me these bills? I help take care of my son!" I offered.

My grandmother didn't have an answer or a solution. At the time, I was employed on a work-study program at school and I was only making about $100 a week. If I paid $75 a week to child support, that would only leave me with $25 a week to live on. I put the envelopes with the bills in them in my top dresser drawer and forgot about them. Two and a half years later, right after graduation, my grandmother called me over again.

"I've been saving these bills," she said. "You should make a court appointment to see a judge about these invoices. I know you've been trying to raise Deshaan and going to school, but this is serious. Child Support has been billing you $75 a week for the past couple of years."

The next day, I made an appointment to see a judge. I was sitting in a courtroom with a judge and two representatives from Social Services, but no one from Child Support. I told the judge that for the past couple of years I only made about $100 a week. I stressed that I also helped to take care of my son. I showed my pay stubs and receipts for miscellaneous things I bought and did with Deshaan.

The judge looked over the documents. "You're 21 years old, you should be doing better," he said. "Until then, I will only demand that you pay $20 a week toward child support."

"Your Honor, I'm going to school, working, and raising my son. How much better do you want me to be?" I asked, "And what about the past-due amount that now totals close to $10,000?"

"I want you to do better in school, find a better job, and be a great dad. We cannot do anything about the past-due amounts," the judge said. "You should have come to us when you first started receiving these bills. Deshaan's mother was receiving Social Services for the past couple of years. This money is due to them for helping to take care of your child. I also recommend you pay $5 a month toward these past arrears."

This experience would be one of my many great spiritual awakenings. The judge was right. It was time for me to do better. I should have been more responsible and not ignored the bills when I first received them. I was slacking in school. I needed a better job. Most of all, I had to be a better dad. Not long after my 22nd birthday, I was ready to start becoming a man. I don't feel the punishment fit the crime, because that one judgment ruined my credit score for at least 20 years. The $5 monthly payments didn't even come close to covering the interest. For years, the judgment would haunt me and prevent me from getting future loans, a good job, a decent vehicle, a house, and an even a respectable apartment. Social Services took my income taxes and would not allow me to save money of any kind, from investing to having a simple checking account. Even though I paid Child Support once a month and continued paying until Deshaan became an adult, it was hard for me to get ahead of the past-due arrears. I neglected to realize how high the interest was and how low my monthly payments were.

I was in the courtroom again, pleading for Family Services to lift the judgment so that it didn't appear on my credit report considering I was paying toward the arrears every month. I was denied. They stated that it would appear on my credit, I would never receive an income tax, I could never own anything that valued over $5,000, and I could never save money until it was paid in full. This made it a little challenging to become a better person.

I remember pleading to a social worker, "I keep my son three to four days a week, I pay child support, and I pay on my past arrears, why are you-all treating me this way? I'm supposed to aim to be a great dad, but I can't buy a home, get a loan, or get a good job, because people are looking at my credit report."

"We know you take care of your son," the woman at Child Support replied. "What you don't understand is that we go by one rule…THE BAD FATHER RULE!"

Once the bank denied us the loan, Carol and I talked about other options. Since her credit was pretty good, I asked her to apply for a loan. She didn't think it was a good idea. We met with a guy from the small business association about our situation and he said if we wanted the business bad enough we would have to do whatever it took, such as using credit cards and applying to other banks.

That night Carol and I talked again about her applying for a loan. We went back and forth for a while before she finally agreed to apply, but the bank denied the loan, saying she didn't have enough credit to get a loan. However, they gave her a line of credit of about $3,500 to purchase items for the store. She then applied for a small-business loan from another bank and was approved for $10,000.

This should have excited us, but it didn't. Carol was frazzled about taking out loans, and as a man, it bothered me, because I felt I should be the one taking the financial risk. Carol and I discussed our roles in regards to running the bookstore full time. She wasn't comfortable leaving Onstar/Sitel. She was worried about her health insurance and receiving a steady paycheck. Carol depended on the security that her job offered because it was what she knew. We agreed I would take the risk, leave Onstar/Sitel, and run the store full time beginning in December. I would also try to get unemployment benefits after I left Onstar/Sitel. It would help me pay my personal bills and act as a contingency fund while running the store.

We met with Megan, our newly-appointed business counselor later that week. She was a white woman around 50 years old with a striking smile. She listened to us for 15 minutes, took a few notes, then paused for a moment, and began to give us advice. "Why do you want to open a bookstore considering bookstores are becoming a dying trend?" Megan said.

"It's part of my destiny, a calling," I answered.

She paused again, wrote a few things on her notepad, then looked at us smiling. "Why don't you two consider postponing this project for a couple of years? It's difficult out there, especially in the bookstore industry. Find a gift shop or something. Ask them to let you rent some space to set up a bookstand. My point is, try something small first."

I looked over at Carol, who was gazing at the floor. She looked discouraged and scared, as if she had seen a ghost and was about to either scream or cry. For the first time during the process of opening our business, I questioned what we were doing as well. By now it was the middle of the summer of 2004. One night as I sat up and prayed, I spoke to God about this new adventure, and wanted to understand more about who I was supposed to be and what I was supposed to be doing. Most of all, I was worried about Carol. For the first time in my life, I challenged God. I needed confirmation that opening a bookstore was truly something He wanted me to do. I knew nothing about being a small-business owner and most of all, I knew nothing about running a bookstore. I also knew little about books. Prior to my research for the business, the last time I was in a bookstore I was about fourteen years old. I had not been in a library since I was about eleven. Even though I was confident that this was my purpose, I requested that God present me with a confirmation just to validate that opening a bookstore was the right thing to do. I wanted to make sure this wasn't just something I wanted as opposed to something God wanted me to do?

"God, on December 10th, I want two sets of keys—one to the bookstore and the other to a brand-new house," I prayed. This would be my confirmation.

Most religions might not agree with this type of bargaining with God, but it was my way of knowing that if God honored these two things on the day I'd chosen, it would make me a true believer. I started searching for a location for the bookstore and a house. My friend Larry Gaddy came by to see me and announced he had the perfect location to open a bookstore. He told me to pick him up on Friday night and he would take me to the location. That Friday I picked up Larry and we headed to a neighborhood in The Queen City called NoDa (which stands for North Davidson Street). It was hard to find a parking spot because there were so many people out and about in the area.

"It's Art Gallery Crawl Night," Larry explained. "Gallery Crawls take place every first and third Friday. They attract a few hundred people. NoDa is considered the art district of The Queen City, so people come to survey the art, patronize the restaurants, shop, and get drunk."

I immediately fell in love with the neighborhood. Two things attracted me: first, the people. NoDa drew in everyone: doctors, clerks, hippies, artists, and more. I had been in The Queen City long enough to know that the city had a lot of cliquish areas. The University area was for the college students, Uptown catered to the young professionals, and Ballantyne was for the newly wealthy. NoDa was a melting pot where people from all of these areas came together. The second attraction was the appearance that the business owners seemed to work together, like a family. I was focused again although I still wanted confirmation from God that this was the right thing to do. For about four months I aggressively pursued a location in NoDa and at the same time I looked for a new home. On December 10th, 2004, I received the keys to both the bookstore and a brand-new house.

CHAPTER 16

LEARNING TO FOLLOW

Months prior to opening the bookstore I began to wonder how it would look and how we would design it. I prayed for about 10 minutes and all of a sudden, I was calling Carol. While praying, God told me to call the Art Institute. I asked Carol, "Have you heard of a place called the Art Institute?"

She said, "Yes. Why?"

I replied, "I'm not sure why but I think I have to call them."

The next morning I called the Art Institute. "I'm not sure why I'm calling, but we need help designing and marketing a bookstore that is opening in about two months."

The operator replied, "Let me get you someone who can help you. I will transfer you to someone in charge of internships."

We had a small budget. The Art Institute sent us an intern that taught us the fundamentals of buying cheap furniture, how to refurbish it, and how to build certain things, like bookshelves. This was another period in my life where I was at a crossroads of one of the biggest challenges in my life. The spiritual part of me knew that this was the right thing to do, but the human side questioned everything like, what if I fail? How can someone open a bookstore and not know anything about one? How will a bookstore help me promote literacy? For the most part, I kept these questions to myself, because I was fearful of discouraging anyone who was supporting me. I spoke to a friend about a week prior to the grand opening. Dee Wrighten had become one of my best friends here in The Queen City.

"Sometimes I question all this. It's coming along so fast. I never had my own business and I don't know much about bookstores."

"You will be fine. You're so driven and focused. It would take an earthquake to stop you! For the past eight months, you've devoted most of your time to building this business. You know what you're doing. The only reason you're questioning yourself is because you never did it before!" Dee replied.

The day before I opened the store, a friend named Paul stopped by. He entered the store, looked around, and said, "How in the hell are you going to open this place by tomorrow?"

I had just finished helping my intern build the last bookshelf. The store was flooded with sawdust, tools, and unarranged furniture. Although it looked bad, I assured Paul that I only needed a couple of hours and I would be done. Everything was there, it just had to be put in place and cleaned. Three hours later, RealEyes Bookstore was ready to open. RealEyes was surrounded by unique restaurants and art galleries. Most of the businesses in NoDa featured crafty vintage furniture. The bookstore was below one of the Queen City elite "hot spots" that featured great spoken word artists that included members of the Queen City Slam Team. I was around the corner from one of the Queen City most-featured performance centers called The Neighborhood Theatre.

RealEyes had used and new books, small pastries, and coffee. It was welcoming. The bookshelves were black and maroon, they weren't that sturdy, but strong enough to hold all of the books. The store smelled like coffee. During the grand opening, I featured a local, upcoming author. To my surprise, hundreds of patrons came out to support RealEyes.

I ran the bookstore for about a year, but then I returned to questioning my purpose in life. Was it really my destiny to become a bookstore owner? Even though I was excited about the people who came out to support the new bookstore, I didn't really understand how this would help promote literacy. Basically I was just selling books to people who were already reading. I also wanted to support the artists in the neighborhood, so I invited them to set up in the parking lot every first Saturday of the month birthing what I called EclecFest. Over 30 visual artists came to each event to sell their products. One Saturday, a friend and author named Cheris Hodges approached me.

"You're doing a great thing for visual artists, but you're a bookstore owner, why don't you do more for authors?" she asked. "Create an event that showcases authors and promotes literacy."

I couldn't ignore Cheris's statement, because someone else had come up to me that same day with a similar comment, and then another person called the store to say the same thing. By now, I had accepted that God can use other people to send you messages. So that day I prayed and asked God what I should about the latest messages I'd gotten. As I prayed, I felt an irresistible spiritual eagerness to create something called the Charlotte Literary Festival. Just as I had done with the house and the bookstore, I gave God a deadline. This time…two weeks.

"God, I will do whatever it takes, but I need help to give birth to something of this magnitude," I prayed. "I need a person with inspiring credibility and respect." I looked up at the clock when I finished praying; it was almost 3 PM on a Friday. Every night for two weeks I stayed up late searching for an author or authors to feature at the Charlotte Literary Festival. With my being new to the literary world, and fairly uneducated when it came to the who's who of that world, my task was very challenging. I hadn't received a positive response from anyone, which led me to believe there was no hope to create the Charlotte Literary Festival.

Two weeks later, I was going through my emails around 2 PM and I noticed an email from a name that was familiar, but I was unsure why. I opened the email and it had one sentence and a signature: I will help you with your event...Nikki Giovanni. My friend Dany Eason came into the store about 20 minutes later. Dany helped create EclecFest and was prepared to assist with the Charlotte Literary Festival.

"Dany, have you ever heard of a woman named Nikki Giovanni?" I asked.

My friend gave me a sarcastic grin. At the time, Dany was hosting a weekly poetry event upstairs from my store at a venue called The Wine Up.

"Jaz, you don't know who Nikki Giovanni is, really? She's not only one of this century's most respected and celebrated African-American poets; she's also an activist and educator who is committed to the fight for civil rights and racial equality, insisting on presenting the truth as she sees it."

"So do you think she can help us in regards to the Charlotte Literary Festival?" I responded, still not quite getting it.

Again, Dany gave me a sarcastic grin and walked out the store. I went to Google to get more information on Nikki Giovanni. What I found to be so impressive about her was that her poetry expressed strong racial pride and respect for family. She was also a civil rights activist. I thought of how in school we had studied names like Martin Luther King Jr. and Malcolm X, but had not studied names like Nikki Giovanni, Cornel West, Angela Davis, and Dick Gregory. I continued to search online for Nikki Giovanni's publicist. I needed clarification that the email was really from her because: first of all, I didn't recall sending her an email; secondly, the email was so short and blunt that it could have been a hoax; and thirdly, I feared that I couldn't afford her even if it wasn't a hoax! I called Penguin Group Publishing and requested the name of her publicist and was transferred to someone else. A pleasant voice said, "Hello, this is Dee Dee. How may I help you?"

I hesitated briefly and then responded. "Hello, Dee Dee, my name is Jaz. I received an email from Nikki Giovanni indicating that she would be a featured author at an event I have coming up called the Charlotte Literary Festival. I just wanted to reach out to you to confirm and make travel arrangements."

Dee Dee paused for a moment and then said, "I'm sorry, I have no documentation confirming an appearance by Nikki Giovanni for the Charlotte Literary Festival. If she had committed to it, it would have gone through me."

The energy seemed to leave me. "Thank you for your time Dee Dee."

After hanging up the phone, I looked up at the sky and said to myself, I tried! I left the store with my head down. That night I didn't say much to anyone. I just went to bed discouraged. The next day, while at my bookstore, the phone rang.

"Can I speak to Jaz?" A woman said.

"This is him."

"This is Dee Dee with Penguin Group. I spoke to you briefly yesterday regarding Nikki Giovanni. Well, Nikki called me this morning confirming that she has committed to your upcoming event."

The reality of the moment hit me. I was nervous. Could I pull this off? I thought to myself. Since talking to Dee Dee, I had conducted more research on Nikki Giovanni. I had also come to comprehend how much great speakers like Nikki Giovanni cost. Even if for some remote chance I was able to get passed the honorarium, the cost of travel and hotel expenses would still be too much for me. Basically, I was building the Charlotte Literary Festival with faith and $350 in my bank account!

"Thank you so much for this exciting news," I said. "Although, as much as we would like to feature her, I don't think we can afford her."

I was astounded to hear Dee Dee's response. "Nikki made it clear to me to not only waive her honorarium, but she demanded that Penguin Group pick up the tab for travel and hotel expenses."

Words can't describe how excited I was! Immediately, I sent out press releases to the media saying Nikki Giovanni was coming to The Queen City. Notices appeared in all the major newspapers including The Charlotte Observer and Creative Loafing. Everyone wanted to interview the legendary Nikki Giovanni and I had to call Dee Dee at least once a week with a request. Nikki approved every interview request, including a substantial one with NPR, which required that she drive 45 minutes from her home at 7:30 AM to conduct a live, in-studio interview a week prior to the Charlotte Literary Festival. I couldn't believe she committed to such a request!

"I feel like I'm asking Nikki too much," I said to Dee Dee one day. "Am I getting on her nerves?"

Dee Dee laughed, "No. Believe me when I tell you, Nikki Giovanni isn't scared to say 'no.' She wants to help you. Nikki Giovanni is not a hype; she's a movement!"

It was a magical couple of months leading up to what would become the annual Charlotte Literary Festival. For the first time in my life I enjoyed being a promoter. I hit the streets almost every day to tell people about Nikki Giovanni coming to The Queen City. What made it magical was the look in people's eyes when I told them, especially the ones who had seen and heard her before.

Soon after, two other appreciated and admired authors responded to my requests to support the festival: New York Times bestselling author Omar Tyree and noted author Patrice Gaines. Other support came onboard including PBS, Creative Loafing, the Neighborhood Theatre, and more. PBS helped me promote the event by offering complimentary advertising on their station. Creative Loafing did the same by offering me free ad space in their newspaper. The Neighborhood Theatre waived its rental fees. No one could have guessed that at the time I only had about $350 in my bank account. Nevertheless, the first Charlotte Literary Festival took place the summer of 2006. It hosted over 30 vendors and 20 local authors and it attracted over 3,000 people.

Nikki Giovanni, Omar Tyree, and Patrice Gaines would return several times to be featured at other events that I hosted for children and adults. The authors and I got to know one another a little more over the years and I came to enjoy and appreciate their strength and passion for life. Each time one of these great authors did a show for me, they refused to charge me for anything.

One night after a show, while walking Nikki to her car, she said, "Jaz, I'll be in town again in six months. Let me know if you'll need me. I'll work for you, of course, at no charge." Nikki Giovanni stated that she would work for me and at no charge!

My experience with Nikki Giovanni taught me what it took to be consistent and steadfast with my vision, as well as how to be humble and give back. God had affirmed again that I was headed in the right direction. Over the years I've had the privilege of working and sharing the stage with a lot of great speakers and authors including: Cornel West, Dick Gregory, Terry McMillan, Zane, Mary B. Morrison, Michelle Andrea Bowen, Patrice Gaines, Michael Beckwith, Susan Taylor, Susan Jeffers, Chris Gardner, Trina Grier, Malik Yoba, Sonia Sanchez, Mary Monroe, Dale Henry, Sister Souljah, and more. This is the power of attraction: a man from the 'hood that knew nothing about books decided to be a leader and attracted some of the best authors we have alive!

CHAPTER 17

LEARNING TO LEAD

Two weeks before the 2007 Charlotte Literary Festival, I received a call from a local newspaper called The Charlotte Observer. The editor wanted to make an appointment to interview me regarding the festival. That year the festival featured bestselling authors: Zane, Mary B. Morrison, Omar Tyree, Donna Hill, Catherine Coulter, Robert Wilcox, and many more. The editor expressed how much she appreciated what I was doing and said she wanted to attract more people to the event.

The day she came to my store I was busy trying to fix a leak in the café area in the back and had to cater to customers near my counter in the front of the store. The editor sat at a table in the middle of the store and asked me questions as I floated back and forth. She asked me a few things about myself. Normally I wasn't comfortable talking about my past, but this day was unusual and I was distracted by anxiety over other things going on in the store.

Halfway through, she stood in front of me, put a hand on my chest, and said, "I don't believe half of the stuff you told me."

I didn't recall everything I had told her, but I knew that whatever it was it had been the truth.

"Can I call a few friends and family members and interview them?" she asked.

Still distracted by the noise in the store, I ran over to the counter and located my cell phone. I gave her numbers for about ten close family members and friends I grew up with.

None of this really sank in until days later when my sister called me and told me she was interviewed by an editor from The Queen City. What did I do? I thought to myself, What had I said?

The following Sunday there was a two-page article in the paper that would dramatically impact my life once again. A couple of my friends told me how surreal it was for me to own a bookstore, because of violent I used to be. I felt naked and embarrassed, so I decided to hide out for a couple of days, however, I couldn't hide for long. The article sparked requests for interviews from all types of media—radio, television, magazine, and other newspapers as well as speaking engagements at local schools. I was not comfortable talking about my past until I had an interview on a talk radio show in Durham, North Carolina. When the interview was over I looked around and everyone in the studio was crying. I had an hour and a half drive back to The Queen City. I vented to my girlfriend Angie about how uncomfortable I felt discussing my past.

Angie said, "It seems as though God wants you to tell your story. Why are you challenging Him?"

"It's not that I'm scared to talk about my past, I just feel like everyone has a story, so why is mine so important?"

"Jaz, you're right. Everyone has a story, but God wants you to tell yours. If your story can inspire and change someone's life, why fight it? This is part of your journey to become a leader, so lead."

The following day I let Angie use my car to go to work while I caught a bus to a local school to speak. I walked into a classroom and noticed a bunch of articles they had of me on a bulletin board. I was staring at the bulletin board when a little girl about nine years old, with small braids and colorful beads hanging from them pulled on my shirt and said, "You a celebrity, huh?"

I thought to myself, Celebrities don't have to catch a bus. But I replied, "I'm no celebrity."

"Well, you're a celebrity to me," she said.

Shortly after that day I was sitting in my bookstore and a customer in the store asked me if I had watched a documentary called The Secret. I hadn't. The same customer returned a few days later with The Secret and insisted that I watch it. It didn't look or sound interesting, although that night I decided to watch it. Carol and I had broken up and I was dating Angie then. The pressure of starting a business together overwhelmed our relationship, along with the fact that I mainly ran the store, which became a major issue with Carol. She wanted to be in the store more often, but again, she didn't want to leave the security of her job. She didn't care for the attention I received from the media and the fact that I was projected as the face of the business. I decided to watch the documentary at Angie's apartment while she cooked one day. When it ended, I ran downstairs. excited to tell her about the movie.

"Angie, you have to see this documentary called The Secret! I finally understand what I'm going through!" I was breathless. "A person can will what they want in life. God blessed us with godly powers to pursue his desires, to follow his purpose. The Secret outlines the Power of Attraction!"

It made me feel better to know there were others out there who were going through what I was going through. I saw a man in The Secret named Michael Beckwith. I admired his views and decided to look him up on the Internet. I thought to myself, I would love to feature him here in The Queen City. During this time, there was a lot of media attention regarding an issue in Jena, Louisiana. The case was nicknamed Jena Six.

For the first time in years, I witnessed blacks organizing a march and I wanted to be a part of it. I sent out a few emails letting some folks in The Queen City know I was going to provide a small bus to Jena. A friend named Messie reached out to me and stated that her mother, Mary Little, had a non-profit organization called Holla and they were willing to offer assistance. They helped cover expenses. The 14-hour drive to Jena was brutal. It was long and tiring and I didn't really understand the connection it had to what I was trying to accomplish with the bookstore at that time. Once we arrived, I witnessed thousands of blacks organizing and protesting peacefully in the streets.

I came across a friend from The Queen City named John who I used to work with. He had stopped by the store once and we talked about the Power of Attraction. John told me that Michael Beckwith, one of the guests on the documentary The Secret and someone I wanted to ask to come to The Queen City, was there in Jena for the protests. John went on to say that Michael Beckwith gave him a free CD and his card.

"Why did he give you his card?" I asked.

"Dr. Beckwith just said one day I would need it," John replied.

I was too hot and exhausted to walk down the street to meet Beckwith.

Once we got back to The Queen City, I called John and asked for Beckwith's number. I called him, but got the answering machine for his assistant, so I left a message. I wanted to see if Beckwith would be the feature at the 2008 Charlotte Literary Festival. By then, the Festival had evolved and we were receiving some sponsorship funding. Still I didn't think we had the resources to afford a name like Michael Beckwith.

A couple of weeks later, I received another surprising call. The woman on the other end said, "May I speak to Jaz?" I looked at the caller ID, which read Rickie Beckwith!

"Hello, Mrs. Beckwith, this is Jaz," I said.

"Call me Rickie. My husband and I received your voicemail. We have one of our leading conventions on the same weekend as your festival. I told my husband that there was no way we would be able to attend your event, but he insisted that we commit to the Charlotte Literary Festival. Not only will my husband be a feature at the festival, but I'm coming as well."

I knew that Rickie Byers was a popular gospel singer, so this was a double honor. Again, I was first excited and then concerned that I might not be able to afford them.

"Rickie, I would love to have you both at the 2008 Charlotte Literary Festival, but I'm not sure if we can afford you," I replied.

"Well, Michael was concerned about that and he told me to tell you to give what you can. We will not demand that you pay our normal honorarium."

Not too long after that call, I received an autographed copy of a book and a small note from a name I recognized. The note read, I received an email from a fan about you. The fan included articles about you and how my book changed your life. I am now a fan of yours. Here's a signed copy of my book and if you have any questions or concerns, feel free to contact me. It was signed, Susan. Susan Jeffers, the internationally-renowned, best-selling author and sought-after public speaker was a fan of mine! Susan Jeffers committed to the 2008 Charlotte Literary Festival. She didn't charge me a penny to appear! It was dreamlike for me to see the person on stage that authored the first book I ever read cover to cover and the book that changed my life.

Since Susan was coming, I decided to reach out to Dale Henry, author of The Proverbial Cracker Jack Box, How to Get Out of the Box and Become the Prize, which was the third book I ever read from front to back. Mr. Henry also committed to being featured at the 2008 Charlotte Literary Festival. Everything was coming together. A year prior to the 2008 Charlotte Literary Festival I had the pleasure of befriending New York Times bestselling author Mary B. Morrison. I decided to ask her if she would return. I featured Mary B. Morrison a year prior at the 2007 Charlotte Literary Festival. She agreed. Not only did Mary B. agree, but she gave me contact information for an elite publicist from Grand Central Publishing named Linda who would later become a great ally.

Linda negotiated bestselling authors Michelle Andrea Bowen, Karrine Steffans, and others for the 2008 Charlotte Literary Festival on my behalf. Grand Central Publishing paid for all of the authors to participate with the exception of Karrine Steffans who required a small honorarium. Soon after, bestselling author and former Essence Magazine editor Susan Taylor agreed to participate. Susan Taylor would also become a powerful advocate that brought something spellbinding to what I was trying to do. The skin of a goddess, perfectly-braided hair, and a diva presence that only legends can present, Susan Taylor was electrifying. She wore a purple gown that gave the impression of her having wings when she raised her arms. When she spoke, the crowd appeared to be mesmerized by her words and inspired by her vision. Almost 8,000 people showed up at the festival to welcome this amazing lineup of authors and speakers. I was truly pleased with the work we had done to make the festivals successful.

One of the most impressive leaders I have met in NoDa is a man that most people who read this book will probably never know. I met Charles Edwards when he became a regular at my bookstore. He came in almost every day for nearly seven years. Charles lived in a small apartment near NoDa and ran errands for many of the local business owners who tipped him a few dollars for each trip. In return, Charles used his earnings to buy food for others in the neighborhood who could not afford it. He even brought me a sandwich sometimes. It was like he had a sixth sense and could tell when I was working long hours and hadn't stopped to eat. People in the neighborhood nicknamed Charles " The Mayor of NoDa."

One day, Charles shared with me how he had been a former crack head. Long ago he was considered a nuisance to the residents of NoDa. He told me that on a few occasions, local business owners chased him down the street waving a gun. He pointed out an old, boarded-up, and abandoned house that he lived in for over two years. Today, at 58, Charles takes several medications daily for his blood pressure, pain in his surgically-replaced knee, and for a mental illness. In spite of a medical condition that he could use as an excuse, Charles gets out of the bed every day to go help others. He reminds me that all leaders don't leave the 'hood, that some give back by staying close to those they can relate to and assisting without complaining.

That's what I wanted to be, a leader that still visits the 'hood on a regular basis, hands on! I respect the leaders that come to my events and I understand why they became an icon, but I'm not interested in being an icon, at least not anymore!

It was time to prepare for the 2010 Charlotte Literary Festival. With only three months to organize, I met with a friend named Shannon. Shannon was a promoter for Neo Soul events. He proposed that we combine the Charlotte Literary Festival and a Neo Soul Music Festival. At first I was hesitant. The angel on my left shoulder whispered in one ear, "Don't do it. That is not why you started all this. The Charlotte Literary Festival is a movement…it's about literacy!" The devil on my right shoulder said, "This is a great opportunity and you can make a lot of money doing it!" Of course, I listened to the devil on the right shoulder and agreed to partner with Shannon. He arranged to bring in at least three featured Neo Soul artists and I agreed to bring to bring in at least three featured speakers/authors. With only three months to prepare, we had to find a location, vendors, sponsors, artists, staff, and more. I felt we could get most of what we needed, but the sponsors would be a challenge. See, prior to Shannon's proposal, I wasn't going to do the 2010 Charlotte Literary Festival. The economy was in the midst of crumbling and it was becoming harder and harder to find sponsors, but up to this point, I had managed to save some money. I figured I would make my money back and hopefully more, because the festival had a pretty good following.

In less than a month, I had three commitments…Susan Taylor, Sonia Sanchez, and Mary Monroe. Almost simultaneously, Shannon had contracted his three featured artists: Algebra, N'Dambi, and Dwelle. This was good and bad news! The good news was that we had a great line-up. The bad news was the collaboration was going to cost more than we expected! After going over the numbers, I anticipated that we would need at least 500 people to purchase tickets just to break even. I didn't think it would be that challenging considering the festival averages over 2,000 people a year. Nevertheless, a couple of days before the festival, I began to regret my decision to move forward and became fearful of the enormous undertaking I'd committed to since I'd gambled every penny I had!

The day of the festival, the artists showed up. The people didn't! Only about 150 people came out to the event. Not only did I spend all my money, but I was now in debt as well. I didn't know how to face everyone. I was ashamed, embarrassed, and broke. I went through the denial stage, then the anger stage, and then the acceptance stage. During the denial stage, I didn't understand how this could have happened to me. I questioned myself, Did I charge too much for the tickets? Did we do enough promotions? Did I give it my all? I just couldn't accept that this had happened to me! I was the good guy! I was the guy running around promoting literacy as if God had honored me to do so!

During the anger stage, I was mad at everyone who helped me. I blamed them for my failure. I met with the team a little over a month after the festival. Enraged, I pointed out everyone's faults and weaknesses. I told the financial expert that she didn't warn me that we were spending too much. I told the person in charge of promotions that she didn't do a good job with promotions. I told Shannon that he should have picked better artists! Most of all, I was mad at God!

As I had done so many times before, I was once facing another crucial time in my life!

After that meeting, I went into hibernation for three months. I refused to answer my phone or emails with the exception of close family members like my son, my mother, and close friends. I was beyond angry at this point. I was mortified. I literally spent all of my money! Of course, I still had RealEyes Bookstore, but it wasn't doing well financially at this point. The book industry was taking a huge blow from the more advanced technical devices like Nooks and Kindles. I decided to close RealEyes, and all of a sudden, I had no income!

I used to wonder how rich people could lose everything so quickly. Although I wasn't rich, it would be the first time I saw so much money go so fast. The festival wiped out most of my bank account. I had a few thousand dollars left, but between my personal rent and all of RealEyes Bookstore's expenses… it was gone within two months. I started receiving eviction notices from the apartment development I lived in. I used to send out a monthly online newsletter at RealEyes. The newsletter informed the public of resources like how to find free healthcare, how to find free legal help, and most of all, I provided information on organizations that helped people who couldn't pay their rent. Now here I was needing the services myself. I called a local company that gave money to people who received eviction notices. They told me that I had to come down to their establishment to apply. I arrived at the location, and I had to stand in a line that took about three hours to make it to the door. I was scared that someone would notice me. I had been featured in several newspapers and local radio stations. The media was attracted to my story…the thug who didn't pick up his first book until he was 30 years old and soon after opened a bookstore. I didn't normally wear hats, but that day I wore one that suspended down close to my eyes making it hard to see my whole face. I was embarrassed because I felt so many people looked up to me and here I was begging for money!

Three hours later, and, almost to the door, a woman came out and told us, "If you only received an eviction notice, you will have to come back another day. Those who have been asked to leave their premises by the Sheriff can stay in the line. We have reached our limit for those who just received an eviction notice."

This was devastating! Not only had I waited in line for three hours, but it was raining! The next day, I decided to get up earlier, so I would have a better shot of getting in, but again, after waiting about three hours, a man came out and repeated the same thing again, "If you only received an eviction notice, you will have to come back another day. Those who have been asked to leave by the Sheriff can stay in the line. We have reached our limit for those who just received an eviction notice."

This time, I decided to wait until I got a letter from the Sheriff to return. A week and a half later, around 5:00 AM, I went back to wait in the line. I prayed that I would make it, because now I was at a point of no return. If they didn't help me, I would have nowhere to live. Four hours later, I walked up to a security guard and he demanded that I fill out an application. He handed me a clipboard with the application and a pen attached to it. He then insisted that I take a seat while filling it out. I asked him, "How long will it take given I've already waited in line for over four hours?"

He responded, "About two to three hours more."

Once I sat down, I noticed an old black woman staring at me. She sat directly in front of me. I returned the application to the security guard when I finished filing it out. As I sat back down, I looked up at the woman and asked, "Do I know you?"

"No, but I know you. You're that guy who does the Charlotte Literary Festival!" she responded.

"Yes, I am," I replied.

"You look embarrassed to be here. You shouldn't be. Most things are seasonal. God wants to humble you. He's not punishing you, but helping you become the leader you were destined to be. These lessons will either cripple you like some tragic events do to people or it will inspire you to evolve and be great! You can't stop believing. Your faith is being challenged right now. I heard you speak before at your festival. You stressed the importance of believing even when the storm comes. The storm is here, do you still believe?" She asked with so much hope.

"Well, I-I'm not sure. I lost all my money. I'm not sure what to do!" I replied.

"You're focusing too much on what you lost and the obstacles it would take to build it again. You just have to believe. Close your eyes. Visualize how it would look to build your empire bigger and better. Don't worry about the money right now. Picture building a better RealEyes Bookstore and an event that will not only just inspire The Queen City, but inspire the world!"

I closed my eyes. I thought back to the conversation my son and I had. DeShaan congratulated me during the 2008 Charlotte Literary Festival. Over 8,000 people came out.

He said, "You should be proud."

I wasn't! After looking over the surveys, I saw that most of the customers were readers. My goal was to attract non-readers. My mission was to convert a community of non-readers into people who were attracted to knowledge. My son responded, "Dad, you don't do anything for non-readers. Also, a non-reader isn't going jump at the opportunity to go to a bookstore or literary event! You have to create something that appeals to non-readers."

I opened my eyes and stared at the woman briefly and asked, "Who are you?"

"I'm a minister. Our church is suffering a little right now and it's affecting our home. My husband suffered from a major injury recently. I know it's seasonal. So I came here to ask for help," she responded.

Not too long after, a woman from behind the counter called the older woman. She got up and told me to give her a hug. I stood up and hugged her.

She whispered in my ear, "You're meant for greatness. I dreamed we would talk one day. You go home and you meditate. Take a shower, turn off the lights, the television, and stereo. Put your head under the stream of water. Focus on what God wants you to do. Then listen."

She walked up to the counter and I never heard from her again. Two hours later, they finally called my name. The organization agreed to help me with my back rent, but it was up to me to find another way to pay the next month's rent. I did exactly what the old woman instructed that night. I made sure it was silent around my apartment. I turned on the shower, took off my clothes, turned off the light, got in the shower, and just listened.

I closed my eyes and saw it. It was beautiful. It had different cultures mingling, vintage furniture, art on the walls, books, and more. I could smell the coffee brewing and hear the large crowd laughing and socializing. Then, I heard a Voice. It told me not to worry about money or how I was going to make this vision come to life. It told me to just continue to listen. The Voice commanded that I first wake up out of my hibernation and visit a friend tomorrow. All of a sudden, I remembered I was in the shower. It was like I was in another world or outside my body. I stepped out the shower, confused. Was that just my imagination? I asked myself. I walked into my bedroom and noticed someone had texted me. It was a friend that I hadn't spoken to for at least three months. She said she called to see if I was alright and asked me to join her and her family for dinner the next night. I responded to the text, I'll be there. I wasn't really excited to go anywhere considering I'd been hibernating for three months, but I met with my friend Aisha the next day.

It was a causal dinner with her family. After dinner, we went into her den and discussed our futures. I heard the doorbell ring. Aisha gave me a look that made me suspicious as she went to answer the door. Seconds later, she returned with a friend named Reika. I had met Reika at RealEyes Bookstore a year prior. When we first met, she wanted me to give her advice on how to start a bookstore because she was interested in opening one. She volunteered at the 2010 Charlotte Literary Festival and soon after that she asked me if I wanted a partner. At that time I wasn't sure what I wanted, but never the less I agreed to partner with her. So while at Aisha's, Reika inquired about our business partnership. I told her that I had to close RealEyes Bookstore due to financial hardship.

She went on to say, "Well, let's build a bigger and better RealEyes Boosktore."

I responded, "Well, I can't afford to." I paused and thought back to the shower experience I had the night before. I had to have faith.

I stood up and said, "Let's do it!"

Aisha, apparently satisfied with her accomplishment, said with a smile on her face, "You two should open one by that popular bakery in NoDa called Amelie's French Bakery. Its open 24 hours a day and it stays packed 24 hours a day."

I decided to explore the area around the popular bakery. Amelie's was located in a strip mall only a couple of blocks away from where RealEyes Bookstore used to be. I entered the atrium and immediately noticed a vacant room for lease. I approached the locked door and realized the broker that helped me get RealEyes Bookstore had showed me this space first. As I peered through the glass door I heard a man call my name.

"Jaz——Jaz, how are you?" The man yelled.

He had to be about 60 years old. He looked familiar, but I didn't know his name.

"I'm Bill. I own Amelie's. I've been watching you from a distance for the past few years. I love what you do in the community. You seem to like this space. It would be cool for you to bring that energy down here" he said.

I responded, "Hello, Bill. I would love to open another bookstore, but I can't..." I paused again.

Bill intercepted, "Is money an option? What would it take for you to take on this space? You have a lot of friends in The Queen City, Jaz. Don't hesitate to ask for help. A lot of people in this city believe in you!"

"Well, this space seems to be more than twice the size of RealEyes Bookstore. I was barely able to afford the rent up there and this rent is probably twice the amount" I responded.

"How much was the rent at RealEyes Bookstore?" he asked curiously.

"$1,400 a month," I responded.

"Call me tomorrow and I'll see what I can do. I know the owner of this building and he might work with you," Bill suggested.

I followed up with Bill the next day. He told me that the owner of the property wanted to meet with me. A couple of days later, Reika and I met with the owner. The owner agreed to lease the space to us for only $1,650 per month and he gave us two free months. A part of me was excited, but the other half of me wondered how we would get furniture and supplies for a space this big. I met with Bill again. Bill gave me a tour of his bakery. I saw why people loved his bakery so much. He had great pastries, but the environment was so welcoming. All of his furniture was vintage. That gave me an idea. We could buy all vintage furniture as well. It's cheap and could be found at any second-hand store.

Reika had a few thousand dollars to invest. I decided to call a couple of my friends for help, and they agreed to loan me a couple thousand dollars. Next, we had to design a plan. I called S.C.O.R.E. again to help design our business plan. Next I called the Art Institute for marketing and design interns again. I wanted to create a place where all cultures could enjoy each other's company. I wanted to create a multicultural lounge that had books, a bar, snacks, and more. I stayed up one night researching elements that brought different cultures together. Each time, hookahs kept coming up. Hookahs are long smoking pipes that give off vapors from a flavored substance called shisha. They come from Morocco. I decided to include hookahs.

Two months later, Red@28th was born. The atmosphere has comfortable: vintage furniture, snacks, healthy foods, hookahs, a full bar, and most of all…books. At the beginning, Red@28th began to make money.

CHAPTER 18

AND YOU STILL TREAT ME AS A THUG

It was June of 2012. I was laying on my bed obsessing over a letter I received earlier that day. The building that Red@28th resided in had foreclosed to the bank. The bank sent me a nasty letter stating that they no longer wanted Red@28th to continue occupancy in their building. Their interpretation was that I was some thug conducting illegal activities like selling hookahs and alcohol. Prior to them taking over the building, I was told by the previous landlord that the state of North Carolina would not allow hookahs or alcohol to be sold from that space. They were right! I made numerous calls and was told by several state representatives that alcohol and hookahs could not be utilized from that space.

I made a call to the mayor's office and pleaded for assistance. The mayor agreed to write the state a letter on my behalf. Within a week or so, another state representative called me and informed me that they would allow the sale of alcohol and hookahs in the space. The bank didn't care that the state gave me permission. They were stuck on the fact that they didn't want hookahs and alcohol in their building.

I got out the bed and headed for the shower. Normally before I took a shower, I turned off all the lights in my apartment, and quieted any noise like the television and radio. It was important that I had a shower with good water pressure. I would stand in silence and in darkness, put my head under the strong stream of water, close my eyes, and just listen!

This was how I meditated…this was how I listened to God. I didn't ask questions, nor would I think about the obstacles of life. This was God's time to speak and my time to just listen!

I needed silence, because any noise outside of the running water would wake me from the meditation. I turned off the lights and closed my eyes, because even a shadow of light would disturb my meditation.

The Voice I heard was strong and firm. Most of the time, It told me things I didn't want to hear. Where I was weak, It showed me how to be strong. Where I was scared, It taught me courage. When I became selfish, It taught me how to share. What I didn't know, It told me how to find the answer. I prefer to use the name Father, because that's exactly how He spoke to me, direct and nurturing, kind but firm. I would forget I was in the shower. I was asleep, but wide-awake.

Praying is the opposite of meditating, at least that's my opinion. Praying is asking the Father to help. Basically, praying is talking to Him and meditating is listening to Him…again, that's my opinion. But this day in June was different. I was frustrated by the letter from the bank. For the first time since I began meditating, I questioned if meditating even worked! While walking to the bathroom, I thought to myself, this meditating thing could be all in my head. The voice I heard while in the shower might not be the Father, it might just be my imagination. I decided to not only give up meditating, but give up praying as well! The next day, I walked into Red@28th and sat behind my computer. A woman approached me.

"Hello, Jaz. You might not know me, but I heard about a program you have called Kickoff to Writing. Can you tell me more about it" she asked?

"I had a bunch of kids write a short essay on the quote, 'Be the change you want to see in the world' by Ghandi. I'm going to publish a children's book with their essays. The world-renowned Nikki Giovanni wrote a great foreword for it," I responded.

"Well, I have a few students who would love to participate. I'm here today for another reason as well. I have a friend that wants to speak to you. He called me today and insisted that I arrange a meeting with you two," she insisted.

"Why, what does he want to talk about?" I asked.

"I'm not sure," she responded.

"Well, I'm really busy today so tell him to give me a call and we'll set something up."

I heard a voice from across the room, "Hey, girl."

He approached the young lady and gave her a kiss on the cheek and then looked to me and said, "Jaz, you got a moment? I need to talk to you about something?"

"You must be the gentlemen she was just talking about. I'm really busy right now. What did you want to talk about?"

"Well, I just need to tell you about something. It'll only take a few minutes," he responded.

"Again, I have a lot of things going on…I'm really busy."

The man and the woman walked away from my counter as I reached for the phone that luckily, began to ring. It was a friend calling about the Kickoff to Writing Program. She was helping me organize a trip to take all the kids up to Virginia Tech to see Nikki Giovanni, Toni Morrison, Maya Angelou, Sonia Sanchez, and Angela Davis speak. Nikki had reserved 40 tickets for all the kids who participated in my program to listen to them speak. The caller and I went over how we were going to get all the kids up to Virginia and the details of publishing the children's book. Midway through the conversation I saw the young lady leave. Where did the guy go? I wondered.

I was on the phone for about a half an hour. Immediately after I hung up, I saw a face peak from behind a bookcase about 30 feet away.

"Jaz, you off the phone?" he asked with a mischievous grin on his face

I nonchalantly walked toward the seating area where he made himself comfortable. He had one leg up on the coffee table, a book in one hand, and a glass of wine in the other.

"How can I help you, buddy," I asked?

"I need to talk to you briefly. I know you're a busy guy, but it's important…God told me to tell you something."

I stared directly into his eyes and asked, "So God told you to talk to me?"

"I know that sounds crazy, but it's true. Please, just give me ten minutes," he requested.

I sat in a chair in front of him. A lot of people some that might be labeled as "odd" come through my store. I wasn't scared or intimidated by them. Actually, I was intrigued by how far right people would go away from the norm…the status quo. I decided to listen to what the man had to say.

"Well, Jaz, it started a few years ago. My wife and I were only two days away from vacationing in Niagara Falls, New York. I felt an odd pain in my right arm. I told my wife about it and she said that we would check it out after the vacation. A couple of days after returning from The Falls, I was at work and found myself staring at the clock, I felt exhausted, I was ready to go home. I was working for a real estate company. I was preparing for a big sell that would take place the next day. I didn't understand why I was so tired, but I decided to leave the office early. Soon after I got in my car, I got a call from my wife. She told me that my aunt was sick and she wanted me to stop by and check on her. I agreed. I pulled up to my aunt's house and began to repeatedly blow the horn. I was hoping she would come out. I was too tired to walk to the door. About two minutes later, my aunt walked out and approached my passenger door. I asked if she was all right. She looked down in the car and ogled at me for a few seconds before asking me if I was all right. I told her that I was fine and I was here to make sure she was okay. She paused again and asked me to hold on for a minute. Quickly, she turned away and ran back into her house.

After a minute or so, impatiently I began to blow my horn again. I was so tired! A couple of minutes later, she approached my car again and told me that she called my father and an ambulance.

'What!' I said in shock. 'Why would you do that? I'm fine.' She responded by stressing that God told her to call my father and an ambulance. We argued back and forth until suddenly I heard a siren. The ambulance was close by. I couldn't help but bark at my aunt for calling an ambulance. The ambulance pulled up in front of my car. My aunt ran over to them while pointing at me. I got out my car to plead my case. I told the driver that I was fine and my aunt was crazy for calling them.

The driver looked me up and down and then asked if he could check me out. I said, 'Hell, no! Nothing's wrong with me'. I also told them I wasn't going to pay for a service I didn't need. The ambulance driver responded by saying that he wanted to look me over and if there wasn't anything wrong, I wouldn't have to pay for the service. I agreed. After looking me over, the driver noted that everything seemed to be fine.

I screamed out to my aunt, 'I told you!'

As I walked away from the ambulance, my father pulled up. He stepped out his car and began to walk toward me and then suddenly he stopped and looked up at the sky. He stood there until I got within a foot or two away from him.

'What's wrong with you?' I asked. He demanded that I get in his car. I replied, 'You must be crazy. I have an important client to meet with in the morning and I'm tired.'

My father grabbed my arm and pulled me toward his passenger door. He opened the door and shoved me in his car. He ran around the car, jumped in, and quickly put the keys in the ignition. The engine roared and his tires sped out as he began racing down North Tryon Street. He drove recklessly while I shouted and complained.

'Why is everyone acting weird today? Why are you driving so fast? What's wrong with this family? I'm fine.'

My dad looked over at me and said that he was taking me to the hospital. He also said that he paused back at my aunt's house, because God told him to rush me to the hospital. Again, 'Is this family crazy? All of a sudden God is talking to you and my aunt about my health? Slow down!'

My dad pulled into the emergency room parking area and rushed me inside. He told the emergency room attendant that I was sick and needed immediate care. The attendant asked my father about my symptoms and all he could say is, 'Please just look him over.' The attendant looked at me and then paused for a few seconds. She told my father that she would have a doctor look me over. By this time, I calmed down and just went with the flow. I called my wife and told her where I was.

Two hours later I was being prepped for a CAT scan. After the CAT scan, I returned to a waiting room to see my wife and kids waiting for me. I assured them I was alright. The kids and I began to talk about school while we waited on the results. Twenty minutes later, the doctor walked into the waiting room. He approached my wife first. He whispered in her ear and all of a sudden my wife began to cry. She didn't just shed tears, she almost lost her balance. At that moment, I knew it was serious.

The doctor walked over to me and told me I had Aortic Dissection and I needed to go into surgery immediately. I was familiar with this condition because I was a fan of the late John Ritter and I knew that Aortic Dissection had been the cause of his death. I also was clear that most people didn't survive this condition. I walked over to my family and hugged them. I began to tell them that everything was going to be all right, even though I felt that it might be the last time I saw them.

He told me that Aortic Dissections resulting in ruptures have an 80 percent mortality rate and 50 percent of patients die before they even reach the hospital. The doctor continued to say that there wasn't a physician nearby to conduct this type of surgery. By then everyone in the room was crying, including my dad. I walked over to my wife and kissed her. I told her to be strong for the kids. A nurse rushed into the room and announced that she had good news. The news was that a doctor who could conduct the type of surgery I needed was on his way, but he was 40 minutes away. She told us that they had to prep me for surgery, immediately.

I remember the doctor putting the gas mask over my face. As my eyes closed, I began to feel comfortable, at peace and more loved than I ever felt in my life. Maybe I'm dying, I thought to myself. All of a sudden I felt like I was floating. I looked down and saw the doctor and nurses working on my body. I watched from the corner of the room until I heard a voice!

'It's alright, Billy. You will be alright,' the Voice said.

'Who are You? What is going on,' I asked.

'I'm God. I needed to speak with you,' the Voice responded.

Then all of a sudden, I heard a beeping noise. I awoke. I looked to my left and witnessed a doctor putting a sheet over a woman's head. The doctor then told the time and day to the nurses. The woman had died. I began to float again. I looked down and saw my body lying on a hospital bed and again, a Voice spoke out to me!

'I need you to do something for Me,' the Voice requested.

'What? Anything!' I replied.

'People are losing faith in Me. Most don't believe in Me anymore. I need you to remind people about Me. I need people to believe again,' the Voice instructed me.

'Why me?' I asked

'That's not important. What's important is that you listen to Me and follow My instructions. I will come to you periodically," the Voice insisted.

'How? Where? Do I pray?' I asked.

'Turn off everything in your home…music, the television, and the lights. Take a shower, put your head under the stream of water and just listen!'

That night, I meditated again in the shower. I heard His voice again, 'The bank will only take what you're willing to give them. Have faith…believe!'"

The next day, I called the law firm that represented the bank that owned the property Red@28th resided in. They made it clear that they were one of the most powerful law firms in North Carolina and they were protecting a bank that could out spend me.

I told them, "Red@28th is like my child. I will fight for it!"

Rodney, my business partner, called me a couple of days later and mentioned that a lawyer was hanging around Red@28th. He also stated that he told the lawyer about our circumstances with the bank. The lawyer wanted to represent us.

After about two months of fighting for us, the lawyer and I met to discuss the next step. We both came to the conclusion that we would take this situation public if the bank didn't back off. The bank finally agreed to back off and let us sign a new lease. I'm not sure if it had anything to do with the threat to take it public, but Red@28th had won! The only thing I had to do throughout the ordeal was believe…without a shadow of a doubt, I would win!

I lay in my bed that night and reminisced. I thought back to when I used to live in The Falls, New York, being a father at such a young age, the drugs that surrounded me, the dad that deserted me, and the mother that changed her life for me. I saw the brutal fights, the pain, the endurance, and my faith…I had to win. The thug had grown up and become a gentleman. The fighter in me wasn't attracted to hurting people anymore, although it's still there to protect me, not as much physically, but mentally.

I had grown up! I built a million-dollar company from faith and I had a new inspired hunger for knowledge. Will I give up the thug in me? Hell, nah! The thug is my fight, it's my endurance, my hustle, my street smarts, and it's what inspired my passion. The gentleman is what supports my family, my business ethics, it's what makes me give back to my community, and it's my relationships, both personal and business!

I believe that we all have a gift and a curse. We all have something that can make us great and we all have something that can destroy us. The key is balance. In this world there will always be a positive and negative, pro and con, yin and yang. Find balance…tame what can destroy you and motivate what can make you great! Everyone has potential. Don't settle. Require that this game of life gives you everything you desire. Spoil yourself! Be the director of your life, or someone will direct it for you. Focus on what makes you happy. Even in the midst of a storm, focus on what will make the situation better. You don't have to see a solution; you just have to believe.

www.ingramcontent.com/pod-product-compliance
Lightning Source LLC
LaVergne TN
LVHW081538060526
838200LV00048B/2136